Introduction to Textures, Animation Audio and Sculpting in Second Life

Introduction to Textures, Animation Audio and Sculpting in Second Life

by Jeff Heaton

Heaton Research, Inc.
St. Louis

Introduction to Textures, Animation Audio and Sculpting in Second Life

First printing

Publisher: Heaton Research, Inc

Author: Jeff Heaton

Editor: Kerrin Smith

Cover Art: Carrie Spear

```
ISBN's for all Editions:
978-1-60439-002-5 (1-60439-002-6), Softcover
978-1-60439-003-2 (1-60439-003-4), Adobe PDF e-book
```

SOFTWARE LICENSE AGREEMENT: TERMS AND CONDITIONS

The media and/or any online materials accompanying this book that are available now or in the future contain programs and/or text files (the "Software") to be used in connection with the book. Heaton Research, Inc. hereby grants to you a license to use and distribute software programs that make use of the compiled binary form of this book's source code. You may not redistribute the source code contained in this book, without the written permission of Heaton Research, Inc. Your purchase, acceptance, or use of the Software will constitute your acceptance of such terms.

The Software compilation is the property of Heaton Research, Inc. unless otherwise indicated and is protected by copyright to Heaton Research, Inc. or other copyright owner(s) as indicated in the media files (the "Owner(s)"). You are hereby granted a license to use and distribute the Software for your personal, noncommercial use only. You may not reproduce, sell, distribute, publish, circulate, or commercially exploit the Software, or any portion thereof, without the written consent of Heaton Research, Inc. and the specific copyright owner(s) of any component software included on this media.

In the event that the Software or components include specific license requirements or end-user agreements, statements of condition, disclaimers, limitations or warranties ("End-User License"), those End-User Licenses supersede the terms and conditions herein as to that particular Software component. Your purchase, acceptance, or use of the Software will constitute your acceptance of such End-User Licenses.

By purchase, use or acceptance of the Software you further agree to comply with all export laws and regulations of the United States as such laws and regulations may exist from time to time.

SOFTWARE SUPPORT

Components of the supplemental Software and any offers associated with them may be supported by the specific Owner(s) of that material but they are not supported by Heaton Research, Inc.. Information regarding any available support may be obtained from the Owner(s) using the information provided in the appropriate README files or listed elsewhere on the media.

Should the manufacturer(s) or other Owner(s) cease to offer support or decline to honor any offer, Heaton Research, Inc. bears no responsibility. This notice concerning support for the Software is provided for your information only. Heaton Research, Inc. is not the agent or principal of the Owner(s), and Heaton Research, Inc. is in no way responsible for providing any support for the Software, nor is it liable or responsible for any support provided, or not provided, by the Owner(s).

WARRANTY

Heaton Research, Inc. warrants the enclosed media to be free of physical defects for a period of ninety (90) days after purchase. The Software is not available from Heaton Research, Inc. in any other form or media than that enclosed herein or posted to www.heatonresearch. com. If you discover a defect in the media during this warranty period, you may obtain a replacement of identical format at no charge by sending the defective media, postage prepaid, with proof of purchase to:

```
Heaton Research, Inc.
Customer Support Department
1734 Clarkson Rd #107
Chesterfield, MO 63017-4976

Web: www.heatonresearch.com
E-Mail: support@heatonresearch.com
```

After the 90-day period, you can obtain replacement media of identical format by sending us the defective disk, proof of purchase, and a check or money order for $10, payable to Heaton Research, Inc..

DISCLAIMER

Heaton Research, Inc. makes no warranty or representation, either expressed or implied, with respect to the Software or its contents, quality, performance, merchantability, or fitness for a particular purpose. In no event will Heaton Research, Inc., its distributors, or dealers be liable to you or any other party for direct, indirect, special, incidental, consequential, or other damages arising out of the use of or inability to use the Software or its contents even if advised of the possibility of such damage. In the event that the Software includes an online update feature, Heaton Research, Inc. further disclaims any obligation to provide this feature for any specific duration other than the initial posting.

The exclusion of implied warranties is not permitted by some states. Therefore, the above exclusion may not apply to you. This warranty provides you with specific legal rights; there may be other rights that you may have that vary from state to state. The pricing of the book with the Software by Heaton Research, Inc. reflects the allocation of risk and limitations on liability contained in this agreement of Terms and Conditions.

SHAREWARE DISTRIBUTION

This Software may contain various programs that are distributed as shareware. Copyright laws apply to both shareware and ordinary commercial software, and the copyright Owner(s) retains all rights. If you try a shareware program and continue using it, you are expected to register it. Individual programs differ on details of trial periods, registration, and payment. Please observe the requirements stated in appropriate files.

Contents at a Glance

CHAPTER 1: CREATING OUTSIDE SECOND LIFE

- Understanding Textures
- Editing Audio Files
- Choreographing Animations
- Creating Sculpties

Second Life provides many tools in-world which allow users to create their own content. There are many aspects to content creation in Second Life. Very complex objects can be created using Second Life's geometric building primitives. Additionally, these objects can be brought to life by adding scripts. Scripts are small computer programs that tell Second Life objects how to interact with the world around them.

Scripting and building are both accomplished inside the Second Life world. All of the tools necessary for building and scripting are already built into the Second Life client. However, additional content must often be created outside the Second Life client. This content is created using third party software, and then uploaded into the Second Life world. This book explains how to create additional content, which can be used to enhance your Second Life builds and scripts. This book assumes the reader already has a basic knowledge of building for Second Life. Many of the techniques presented are only of use to Second Life builders. For an introduction to the Second Life building process, Beginning Building in Second Life, ISBN 1-60439-004-2, may be useful. For more information on scripting, please see Scripting Recipes for Second Life, ISBN 1-60439-000-X.

Understanding Textures

Textures are very important in Second Life. Without textures, every object in Second Life would appear in a single color. Textures are image files which can be used to "wrap" the geometric primitives (prims) used in Second Life . Since textures are images, they can add a great deal of realism to prims.

Every item in Second Life starts out with a simple wood texture. Figure 1.1 shows a simple box which has had a different texture applied to one of its faces. The other faces display the default wood texture.

Figure 1.1: A Textured Box

Textures are not created inside Second Life. Textures are usually created in a program, such as Photoshop or GIMP. This book will focus primarily on Photoshop. However, one chapter is devoted to explaining how to use GIMP in place of Photoshop. GIMP is a free, open-source, image editing application. Photoshop is a proprietary, closed-source, commercial application. Figure 1.2 shows a typical Photoshop screen shot

Figure 1.2: Editing a Texture with Photoshop

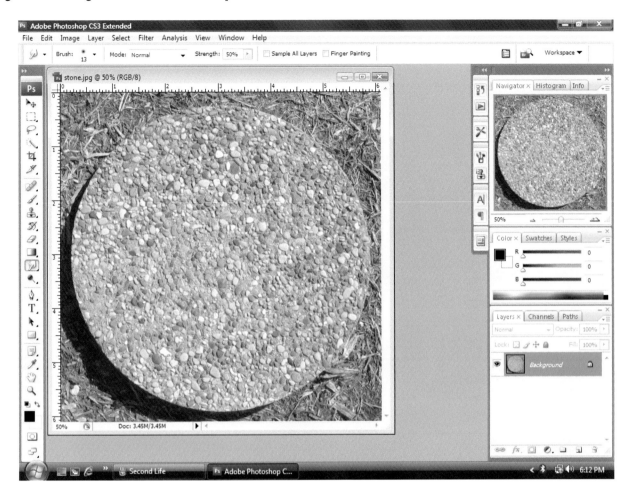

Textures can also be designed to be tiled. A tiled texture can be repeated many times without showing any "seams." For example, consider Figure 1.3.

Figure 1.3: A Tileable Texture

This figure shows a single texture. Because this texture is tileable, it can be seamlessly applied to a large object in Second Life. The tileable texture will simply repeat, as shown in Figure 1.4.

Figure 1.4: A Large Object With Tileable Textures

Tileable textures can be used for more than just tiles. Figure 1.5 shows a tileable texture used to create a large paved area. It is nearly impossible to tell by looking at it, but this paved area is actually a 10 X 10 array of 100 tiles.

Figure 1.5: A 10 X 10 Array of Tiles

Tileable textures can be used for any pattern that needs to be repeated over a large area.

Textures can also include transparent regions. This is done through the use of something called an alpha channel. Figure 1.6 shows a texture with transparent regions.

Figure 1.6: A Texture with Transparent Regions

Textures will be covered in greater detail in Chapter 2, "Textures and Alpha Channels" and Chapter 3, "Tile-able Textures."

Editing Audio Files

Audio clips can be uploaded to Second Life. These recordings can be up to 10 seconds in length. A third party tool is needed to record and edit these sounds before they are sent to Second Life. This book will explain how to use a program called Audacity to edit audio files for Second Life. Figure 1.7 shows how a sound is edited using Audacity.

Figure 1.7: Editing a Sound in Audacity

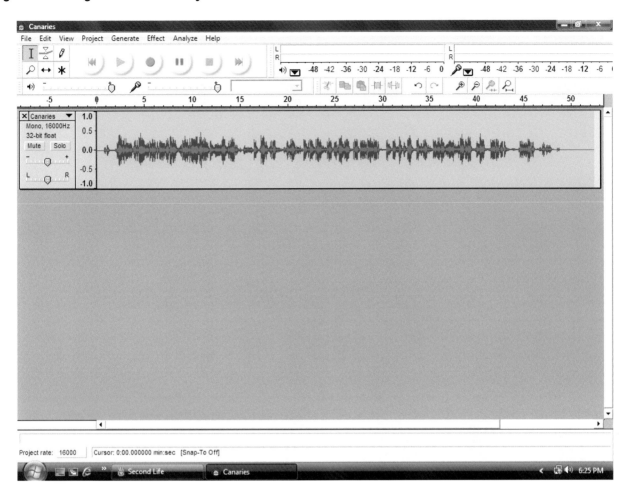

Sometimes it is necessary to loop audio clips. For example, the sound of a running car might be looped for as long as the car remains running. The sound of a car starting would not be looped, because in the real world, the "car starting" sound is heard, followed by a "running car" loop.

Audio files will be covered in greater detail in Chapter 6, "Composing Audio Files."

Choreographing Animations

Animations in Second Life are used to animate the avatars. The avatars in Second Life represent human players. Figure 1.8 shows three avatars standing together.

Figure 1.8: Avatars Standing Together in Second Life

By default, avatars move their arms, legs, and other body parts as they walk, run, and fly about the Second Life world. Animations allow avatars to move their bodies in ways that were not originally programmed into Second Life. Typically, animations allow the avatars to interact with objects. For example, if a canoe were created in Second Life, a corresponding animation would likely be created to allow the avatar to paddle the canoe.

Animations are created in a third party program and then uploaded to Second Life. There are many different programs that can be used to create avatar animations. This book will make use of a free program named Avimator. Figure 1.9 shows an animation being edited using Avimator.

Figure 1.9: Using Avimator

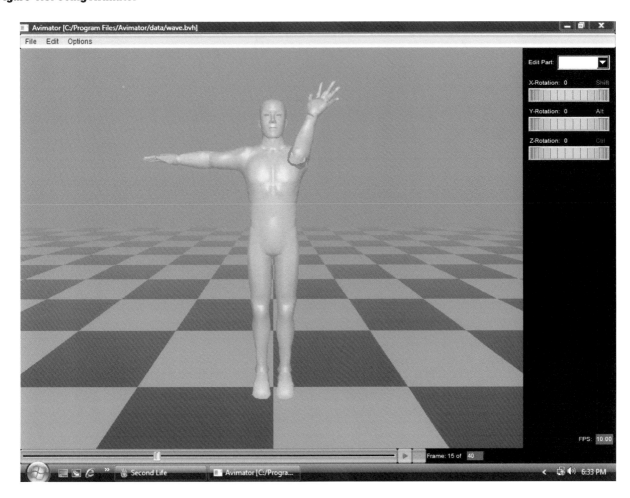

Once an animation has been created, it can be used with an in-world avatar. Figure 1.10 shows an avatar using the animation created in Figure 1.9.

Figure 1.10: An Avitar Using an Animation Created with Avimator

Figure 1.10 shows the avatar posing in a single animation frame. Animations can also be created which cycle through a series of poses, or frames, thereby allowing avatars to act out certain actions.

Animations will be covered in greater detail in Chapter 5, "Creating Animations."

Creating Sculpties

Sculptured prims were introduced to the Second Life world in mid-2007. Sculptured prims are often referred to simply as "sculpties." Regular prims in Second Life are based on one geometric shape, such as a sphere or a cube. Sculpties can be created in third party programs and can involve more complex shapes than those used for regular prims.

Sculpties have two considerable advantages over regular prims. First, they allow curves and shapes which are not possible with regular prims. Second, they allow a single prim to be used rather than several smaller regular prims. Before the creation of sculpties, collections of regular prims were often linked together to create the same effect.

There are a number of third party programs available which can be used to make the shape maps necessary to create sculpties. The program that will be used in this book is a free program called Sculptypaint. Figure 1.11 shows Sculptypaint being used to create a sculpty.

Figure 1.11: Using Sculptypaint

Once the shape map created by Sculptypaint is uploaded to Second Life, a sculpty can be created using the uploaded map. Figure 1.12 shows a sculpty in the Second Life world.

Figure 1.12: A Sculpted Prim

Sculpties will be covered in greater detail in Chapter 7, "Understanding Sculpties."

Summary

Third party programs can be used to create multimedia elements that can enhance building and scripting projects in Second Life. These multimedia elements are created outside Second Life and then uploaded into the Second Life world. These multimedia elements include audio files, sculpties, and textures.

Audio files can be used with scripts to play sounds. These sounds are recorded and edited in a program such as Audacity. These sounds can be looped to produce a continuous sound, such as the sound of a running car.

Sculptured primitives, or sculpties, can be created in external programs such as Sculptypaint. Sculpties allow prims to go beyond their simple shapes. Using a sculpty can reduce the total number of prims needed to create an object.

Textures are very important to the building process in Second Life. Textures allow an image to be wrapped around a prim. Textures can be tileable, which means that they blend seamlessly when the square textures are placed next to each other. Textures can also include transparent regions using alpha channels. Alpha channels will be covered in the next chapter.

CHAPTER 2: TEXTURES AND ALPHA CHANNELS

- Obtaining Textures
- Editing with Adobe Photoshop
- Cropping Images
- Understanding Canvas and Image Size
- Second Life Portraits
- Understanding Alpha Channels

Without textures, Second Life objects would appear very plain. Textures allow images to be mapped onto the surface of Second Life objects. For example, an image depicting concrete may be used as the texture for a sidewalk. The concrete texture causes the sidewalk to appear as though it is made of concrete.

The Second Life library contains many different textures that can be used for building projects. These textures can be found in the textures folder of the main library folder. Figure 2.1 shows some of these textures.

Figure 2.1: Library of Textures

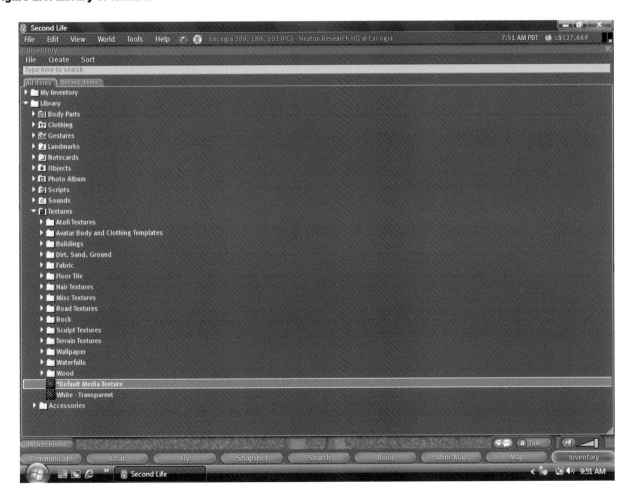

As can be seen in Figure 2.1, the textures library is arranged hierarchically.

Obtaining Textures

The library contains many useful textures, however, for many building projects, these textures will be insufficient. When the built-in textures are insufficient, additional textures may be uploaded to Second Life. This chapter discusses how to create these textures. Creation of a texture follows one of the following procedures:

- Create an illustrated texture from scratch
- Take a photograph with a digital camera
- Download an image from the Internet

While most textures begin with a source image, textures can also be created from scratch, by someone who is good at illustrating objects. Programs such as Adobe Illustrator are useful for this procedure.

The most common source for images is the Internet. Whenever images are downloaded from the Internet, it is important to remember to obtain all necessary copyright clearances. Many images available on the Internet are free, however, some require payment. Other images are not available for use at all. Whenever in doubt about the legal status of an image, always consult an attorney. Obtaining image permissions is beyond the scope of this book.

Using Google Image Search is a great way to find images for textures. The Google Image Search can be found at the following URL:

`http://images.google.com/`

To begin using the image search, enter the name of the type of image sought. For this example, a search was done on "stone texture." Adding the word "texture" to the search is often helpful, as it causes the search to find images that were specifically created as textures. The Google image search will return a list of images, as shown in Figure 2.2.

Figure 2.2: Google Search Results for Stone Textures

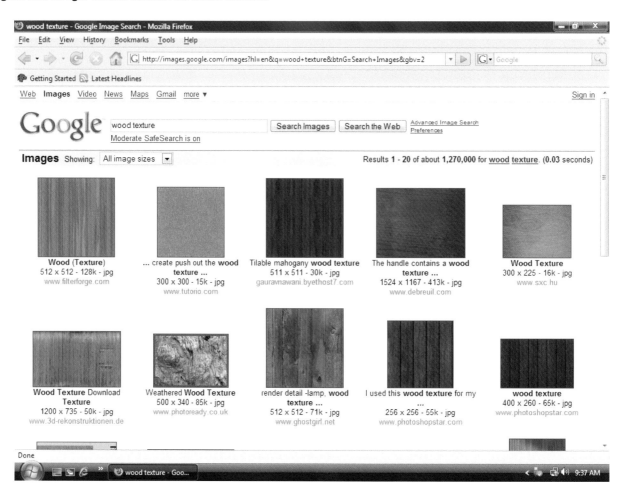

Once a stone texture has been found that looks interesting, click on that texture. This will reveal a screen similar to Figure 2.3.

Figure 2.3: Web Page Containing a Stone Texture

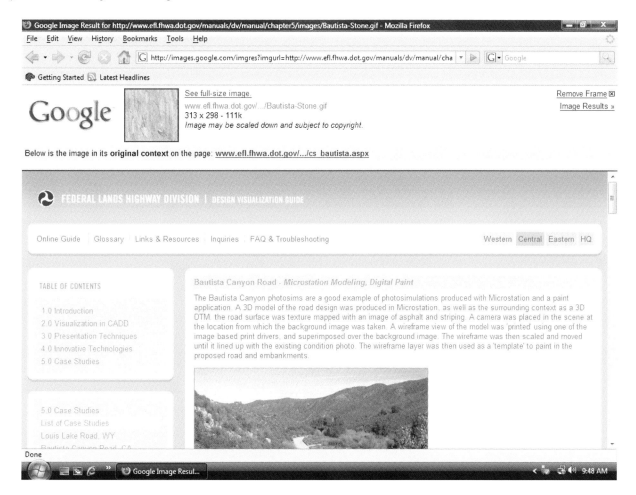

If this image satisfies your requirements, then click the "See full-size image" link, as shown near the top of Figure 2.3. This will display only the image in the browser. Next, select "Save" from the "File" menu to save the image to disk.

Whether the image has been obtained from the Internet or by using a digital camera, it will likely require some editing before it can be uploaded to Second Life.

Editing with Adobe Photoshop

Photoshop is a commercial image editing program produced by Adobe. More information about Photoshop can be obtained from the following URL:

`http://www.adobe.com/products/photoshop/index.html`

This book uses the Adobe CS3 version of Photoshop. While Photoshop is one of the most advanced and widely used image editing programs, it is not the only choice. A free alternative to Photoshop is the GNU Image Manipulation Program, or GIMP. Chapters 2 and 3 of this book will focus on image editing using Photoshop. Chapter 4 will explain how to apply these same techniques using GIMP. If GIMP is the image editor to be used, you should still review Chapters 2 and 3 to understand the concepts behind the editing process.

Entire books have been written on how to use Photoshop. This chapter, as well as Chapter 3, will provide a basic introduction to Photoshop. These two chapters will focus on the features of Photoshop that are the most useful to someone creating for Second Life. This chapter will specifically cover the following techniques.

- Cropping Images
- Adjusting the Canvas and Image Size
- Second Life Portraits

Cropping Images

Cropping is a very important image editing technique. Cropping allows unneeded portions of an image to be discarded. To see how to crop an image, start Photoshop and open an image. A sample uncropped image is seen in Figure 2.4.

Figure 2.4: An Image Opened in Photoshop

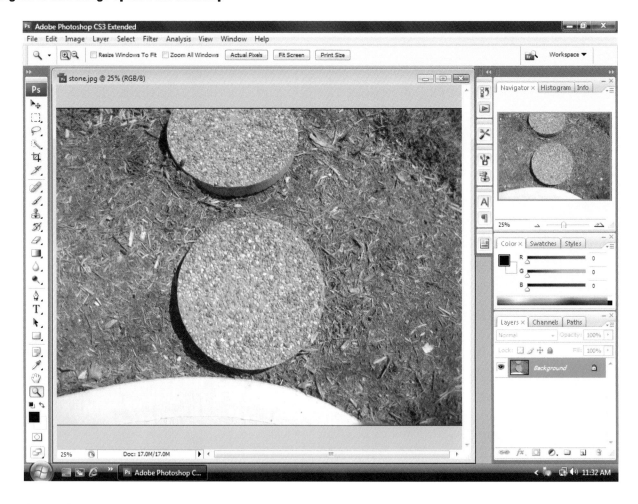

As can be seen in Figure 2.4, there are two steppingstones in the sample image. For this example, the texture desired for inclusion in a Second Life object is the one steppingstone near the center of the image. Therefore, the image needs to be cropped, so it includes just the steppingstone in the center. To do this, you can use the "Rectangular Marquee Tool." Select the tool and drag a rectangle around the steppingstone. Once the rectangle has been drawn, choose "Crop" from the "Image" menu. This will result in the image being cropped, as is illustrated in Figure 2.5.

Figure 2.5: Cropped Steppingstone Image

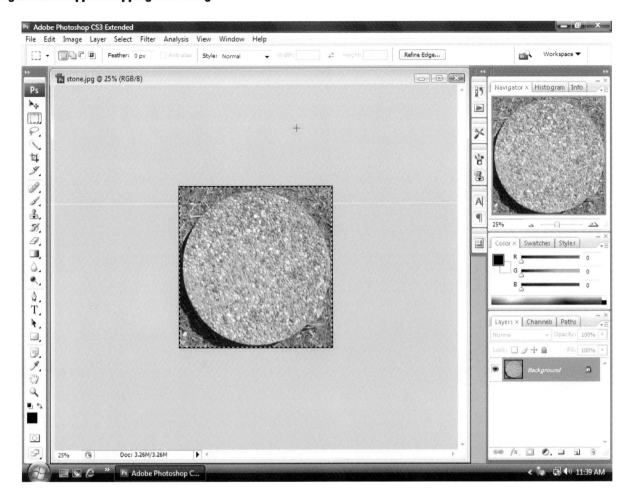

Now that the stone has been cropped, the next step is to adjust its size.

Adjusting the Canvas and Image Size

The steppingstone was photographed with a 6.0 megapixel digital camera. This produced a high-resolution image that is far too big to be used in Second Life. Therefore, the image's size needs to be adjusted. There are two sizing options available under the "Image" menu:

- Image Size...
- Canvas Size...

It is very important to understand the difference between these two operations. Adjusting the image size will decrease or increase the resolution of the image, without discarding any of the image. Changing the canvas size will discard parts of the image near the sides, but will not change the resolution.

If "Image Size" is selected from the "Image" menu, a screen similar to Figure 2.6 will be displayed.

Figure 2.6: Change Image Size

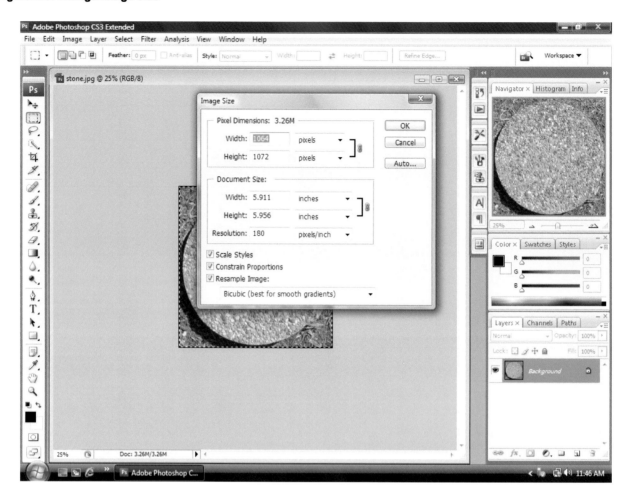

As can be seen in the above figure, the image is 1064 pixels wide and 1072 pixels high. Changing the width to 512 will also change the height. The height is changed to 516, because the "Constrain Proportions" box is checked. This prevents the image from being "stretched." For example, if the 1064 x 1072 image were resized to 512 x 1072, it would be necessary to stretch the image. Resizing to 512 x 516 simply produces a smaller version of the steppingstone, as seen in Figure 2.7.

Figure 2.7: A Smaller Steppingstone

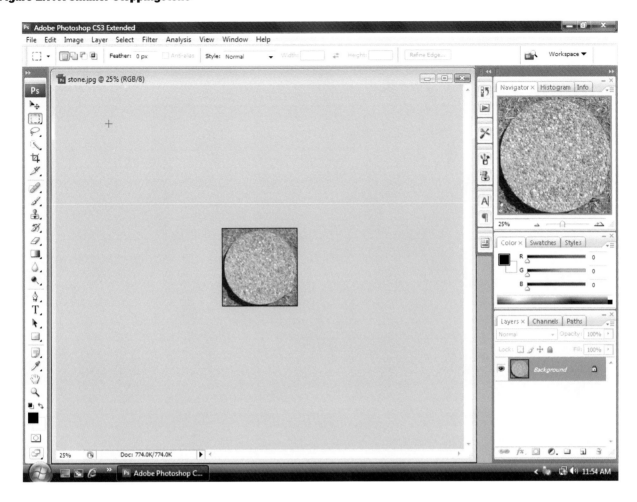

Now consider what would happen if the canvas size were adjusted. When "Canvas size" is selected from the "Image" menu, a screen similar to the one shown in Figure 2.8 is displayed.

Figure 2.8: Adjusting the Canvas Size

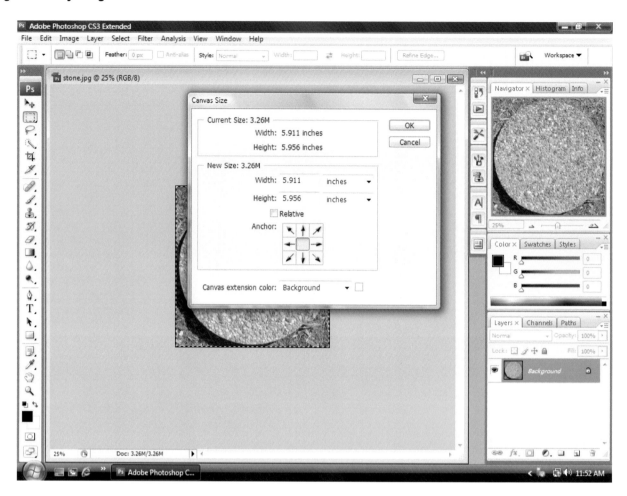

One of the first things to notice about Figure 2.8 is that the units are not in pixels. The units are in either inches or centimeters. Use the pull-down menu to change the units to pixels. Now the width and height can be changed to 512 pixels each. The proportions are not constrained when the canvas size is adjusted. This is because a canvas size change will never stretch the image. Therefore, whatever does not fit on the canvas is simply discarded.

The "anchor" shown in Figure 2.8 is used to specify which part of the image should not be discarded. Figure 2.8 shows the anchor as a 3 x 3 grid of squares. Squares which are selected, represent the part of the image that will not be discarded.

Selecting a value of 512 for both height and width, results in a modified image, as illustrated in Figure 2.9.

Figure 2.9: Adjusted the Canvas Size

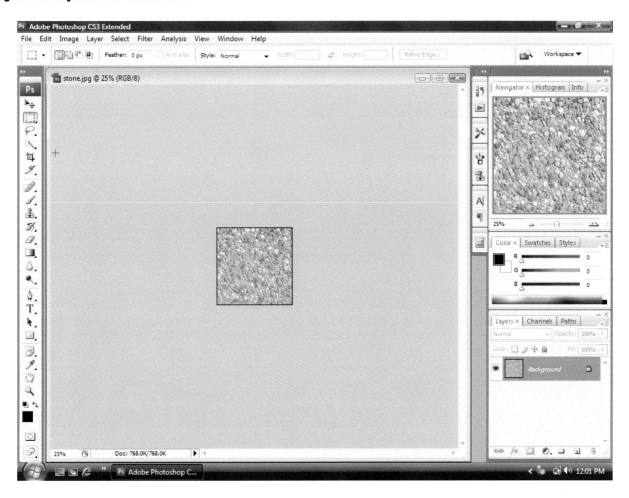

As can be seen, the sides of the steppingstone have been discarded.

Second Life Portraits

Second Life portraits are very popular for profile pages. Figure 2.10 shows Encog Dod's Second Life profile. This profile includes a portrait of Encog Dod.

Figure 2.10: Encog Dod's Second Life Profile

Consider how to take a picture of Encog Dod. First, Encog Dod must be pointing in the correct direction. Usually only the back of your avatar is visible as it walks around. This does not work well for portraits. The camera must be positioned so that it is facing the front of Encog. This is done by selecting "Camera Controls" from the "View" menu. The arrows on the camera control can be used to rotate the camera so the front of Encog is visible.

Once the camera is correctly rotated, Encog can be photographed. Second Life includes a snapshot capability. By clicking the "Snapshot" button near the bottom of the screen, a snapshot will be taken, resulting in an image similar to Figure 2.11.

Figure 2.11: Taking a Snapshot

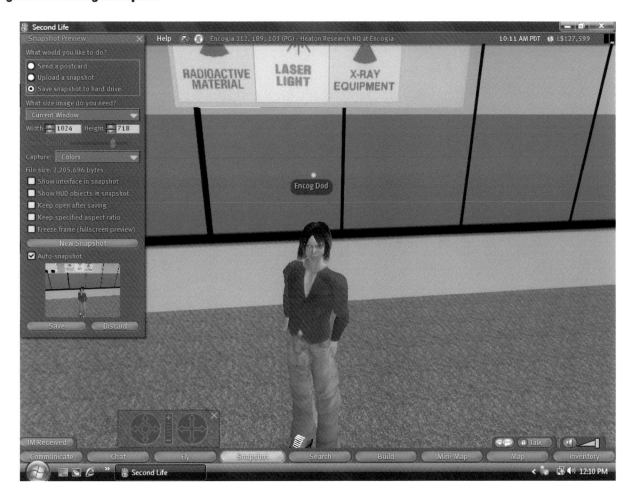

This snapshot is a good image of Encog, but there are several issues to be addressed if it is to be used as a profile portrait. First, the snapshot is not square. A Second Life portrait is always displayed in a square box. If the actual portrait is not square, then Second Life will stretch the portrait to fit the box. For the portrait to look its best, it should not be stretched.

To address this problem, the portrait should be opened in Photoshop. As with the steppingstone example above, you will need to draw a box around the portrait. Try to make the box as square as possible. Once cropped, you will have a nearly square portrait. Now adjust the canvas size, as illustrated in Figure 2.12.

Figure 2.12: Creating a Square Portrait

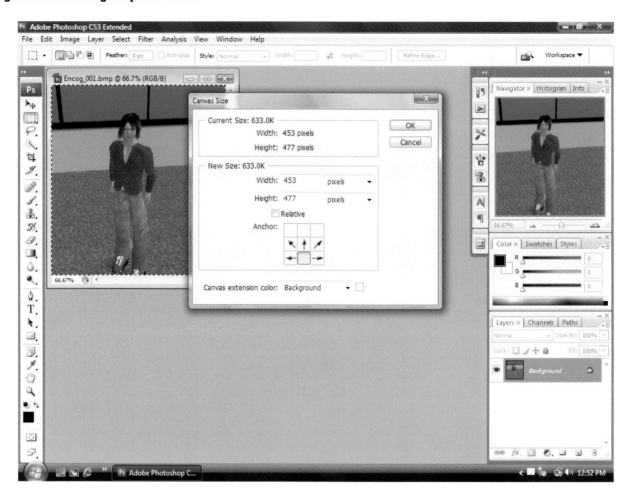

As seen in Figure 2.12, the image is 453 x 477 pixels. The lower of the two values, 453 is chosen, and the height is adjusted to 453. Adjusting the height to 453 will trim off the top and bottom edges of the image. Since there is extra space at the top of the image, above Encog's head, it would be best to trim this space. To do so, the anchor must be moved to the bottom of the image, as shown in Figure 2.12. This will keep the bottom part of the image.

Once the canvas size is adjusted, the image is square. The square image should be saved as a JPEG and uploaded to Second Life. To upload an image to Second Life, choose "Upload Image" from the "File" menu. This will allow you to upload the image, which will then appear in the textures portion of the inventory.

Understanding Alpha Channels

Alpha channels allow portions of an image to appear transparent. Consider a window. A texture could be used to create a realistic looking window. However, it may be desirable to be able to see through the window. To do this, a window can be created using alpha channels to specify which parts of the window should be transparent. First a window is loaded into Photoshop, as shown in Figure 2.13.

Figure 2.13: A Window

This image was taken with a digital camera. It provides a good starting point for a window texture. This window has a total of 12 panes. Six of the panes are on the top and six are on the bottom. To make it easier to select the windowpanes, you should use the zoom function to focus directly on the panes. This does not alter the image, it simply provides you with a better view of the area being worked on. To zoom in, select the magnifying glass on the tool bar and click where the magnification should occur. To zoom back out, hold down the alt key and click while using the magnifying tool.

To create a transparent region, the first windowpane should be selected using the rectangular marquee tool, as discussed earlier in this chapter. Figure 2.14 shows the first pane selected.

Figure 2.14: The First Window Pane

Alpha channels can be created by selecting regions of an image and then saving the selection. The region that is select will be opaque, and the region not selected will be transparent. The easiest way to accomplish this in the windowpanes example is to select each of the panes, one-by-one. Once all of the panes have been selected, the selected regions can then be inverted, so the opaque regions are selected. To invert, choose "Inverse" from the "Select" menu.

Figure 2.15: All Window Panes

Once the correct region of the image has been selected, the alpha channel must be created. To create an alpha channel, choose "Save Selection..." from the "Select" menu. The defaults for the "Save Selection" dialog box can be accepted, as shown in Figure 2.16.

Figure 2.16: Creating the Alpha Channel

To see the alpha channels, select the "Channels" palette. If the "Channels" palette is not visible, select it from the "Window" menu. Click the "Eye" next to the "Alpha 1" channel. This will put red in front of every area covered by the alpha channel, as shown in Figure 2.17.

Figure 2.17: Viewing the Alpha Channel

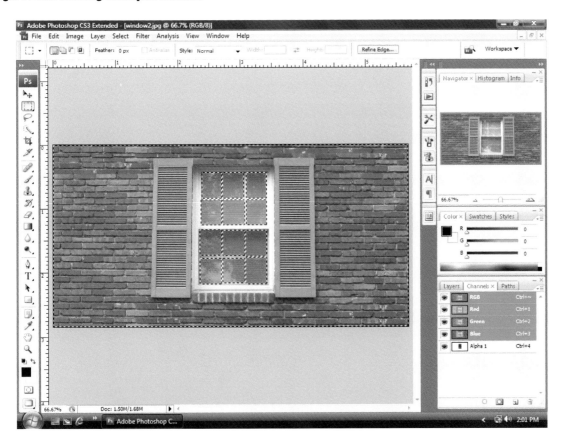

The image should now be saved as a Targa file. Targa is a graphics file format. Targa supports transparency. Select "Save As..." from the "File" menu. Select the Targa file format, as shown in Figure 2.18.

Figure 2.18: Saving the Targa File

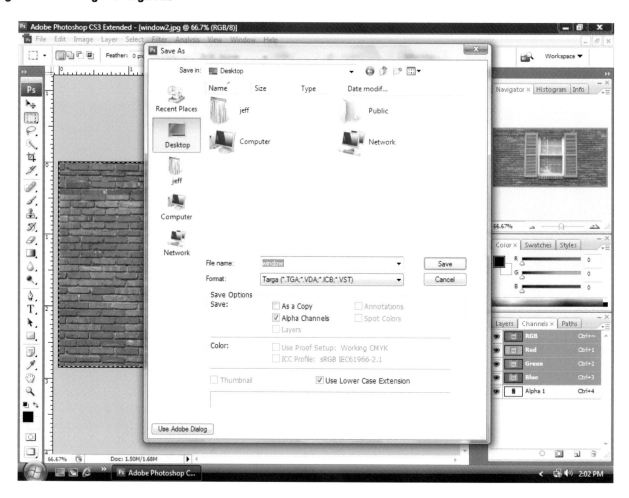

Make sure the Targa file is saved as "32 bits/pixel." Once the Targa file has been saved, it can be uploaded to Second Life. To upload an image into Second Life, select "Upload Image" from the "File" menu. Second Life will display a preview of the transparency, as shown in Figure 2.19.

Figure 2.19: Uploading a Transparent Image

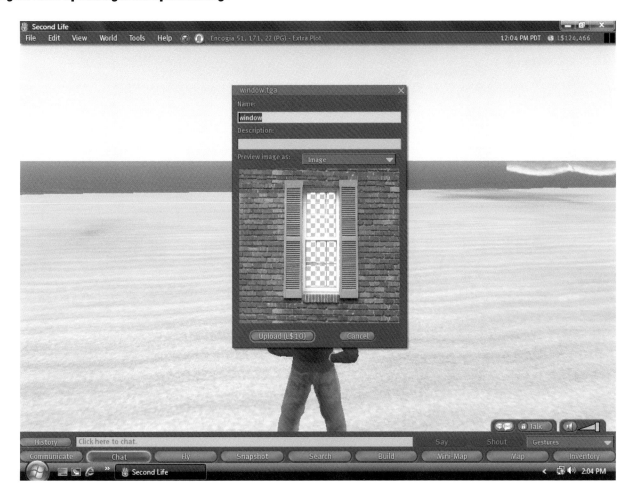

If the transparency looks correct, then choose to upload.

The texture can now be applied to a prim in Second Life. Figure 2.20 shows the texture being used in Second Life.

Figure 2.20: Using a Transparent Texture

The transparent texture allows the user to see through the window.

Summary

Textures are a very important part of Second Life. Textures allow prims to appear realistic. This chapter introduced some of the most common techniques used with Adobe Photoshop to create textures. This included cropping and alpha channels.

Cropping allows unneeded portions of an image to be discarded. The image or canvas can also be resized. When the image is resized, the actual image is stretched to the new size. When the canvas is resized, the parts of the image that do not fit within the new canvas size will be removed. Alpha channels allow parts of an image to appear transparent. Any area selected for inclusion in the alpha channel will appear transparent. This is very useful for creating windows.

Tileable textures can be placed next to each other without seams between them. Therefore, textures can easily be reproduced to cover a large area. The next chapter will introduce methods for creating tileable textures in Photoshop.

CHAPTER 3: TILEABLE TEXTURES

- Understanding Tileable Textures
- Creating a Tileable Texture Using a Non-Patterned Image
- Creating a Tileable Texture Using a Patterned Image
- Using Tileable Textures in Second Life

Tileable textures are a special type of texture that can be tiled. Tiling a texture means repeating the texture in a grid fashion. If the texture is tileable, then there will be no visible "seam" where two textures touch.

Tileable textures are very useful in Second Life, because they can cover large areas. Consider a large grassy field. There is no reason to create one huge grass texture image to cover the entire field. Rather, create one small tileable texture and tile it across the entire field.

When searching the Internet for textures, the ability to tile is an important consideration in deciding which image to use. Many textures found on the Internet are already tileable. However, it is also possible to transform non-tileable images into tileable images. This technique will be discussed in this chapter.

Understanding Tileable Textures

It is hard to look at an image and determine whether or not it is tileable. However, it is quite easy to see why a non-tileable image is not tileable when it is tiled. Figure 3.1 shows an attempt to tile a non-tileable image.

Figure 3.1: A Non-Tileable Image

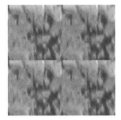

Notice the visible seams above? If a large number of these textures were tiled together, the grid would be clearly visible. The goal of tiling is to create a seamless image, which covers the grid.

Tileable images accomplish this goal. Figure 3.2 shows a tileable image being tiled.

Figure 3.2: A Tileable Image

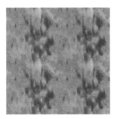

The above image has no noticeable seams. This is the advantage of using a tileable image.

This chapter will now discuss how to create tileable images. The first step is to obtain an image to make tileable. Refer to Chapter 2 for some ideas on how to obtain images. The next step depends on what type of image is to be tiled. There are two general types of tileable images:

- Non-Patterned
- Patterned

A non-patterned image is an image which does not contain a complex pattern that stretches across its entire surface. Grass or sand is a good example of a non-patterned image. A patterned image has complex, but repeatable, patterns. Bricks are a good example of a patterned image.

Creating a Tileable Texture Using a Non-Patterned Image

Non-patterned images are generally easier to work with than patterned images. The non-patterned image that will be used for this example is shown in Figure 3.3.

Figure 3.3: A Non-Tileable, Non-Patterned Image

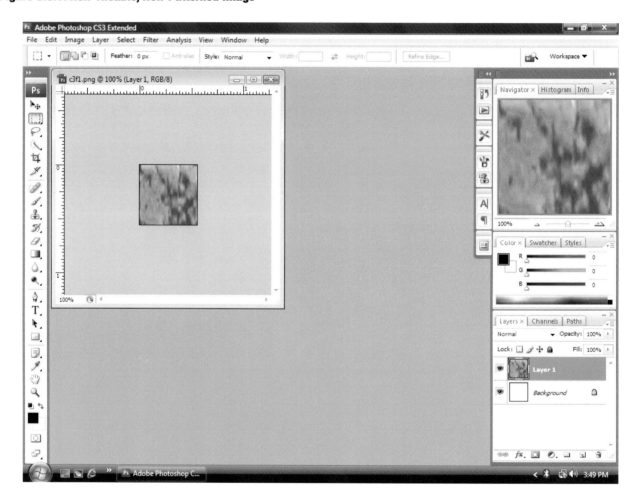

The first step is to make the image square. It is not absolutely required that the image be square, but a square image will be much easier to work with. For a non-patterned image, simply adjusting the canvas size is usually sufficient to create a square image. For more information about adjusting the canvas and image sizes, refer to Chapter 2. For this example, the canvas size is adjusted to 100 x 100 pixels.

Photoshop includes a built in filter that allows the image to be viewed in a way that shows the seams. This allows the seams to be corrected while they are clearly visible. To use this tool, select "Other" from the "Filter" menu. From "Other," select "Offset." A screen similar to the one shown in Figure 3.4 will be displayed.

Figure 3.4: Offsetting an Image

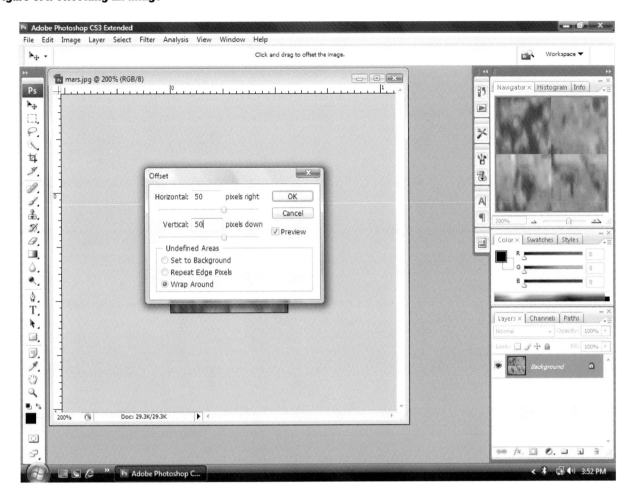

The image should be offset by half of its height and width. Since the sample image is 100 pixels square, it should be offset by 50 pixels, as shown in Figure 3.4. Once the offset is complete, the image will display as shown in Figure 3.5.

Figure 3.5: Offsetting an Image

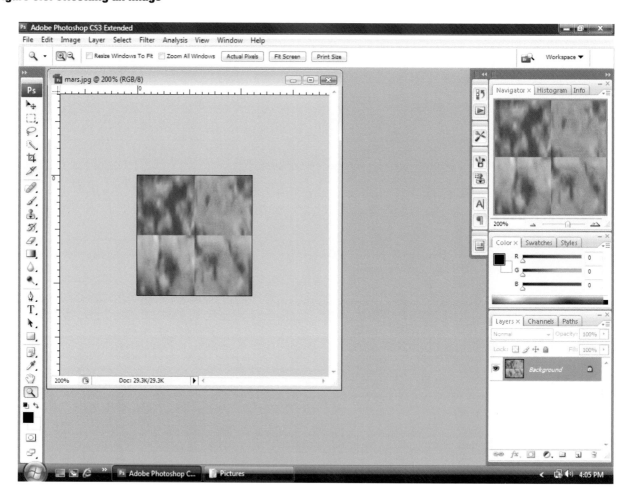

As can be seen in Figure 3.5, the seams are clearly visible. Now the seams should be fixed using one of Photoshop's many tools. A particularly useful tool is the bandage brush. The bandage brush appears on the toolbar as a small bandage. Select the bandage brush, then shift-click somewhere in the middle of an area between two seams. Do not click too close to a seam. Now use the bandage brush and paint over the seams. The seams will be removed. Once the seams are removed, the image will display as shown in Figure 3.6.

Figure 3.6: Seams Removed From the Image

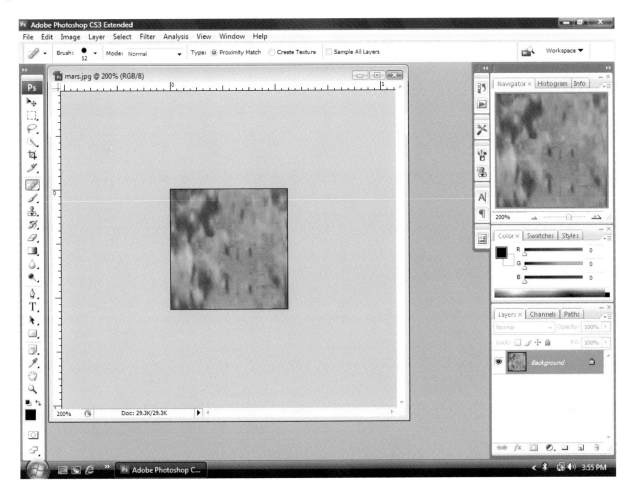

Once the seams have been removed, the offset should be removed. Open the offset dialog box, as described earlier. Enter the same values are before. Repeating this step will remove the offset. The image can now be saved and uploaded to Second Life. Working with a tiled image inside Second Life is covered later in this chapter.

Creating a Tileable Texture Using a Patterned Image

A patterned image is one that has an underlying pattern to it. Creating a tileable patterned image is not as easy as creating a tileable non-patterned image. For this example, a brick texture will be created. The brick texture example in this chapter was obtained using a digital camera. The first step is to crop a region of the image that repeats. This will form the basis of the texture. Try to choose a square region that repeats. The repeating region will usually not be a perfect square and the image will need to be resized to make it square. Image resizing was covered in Chapter 2. Figure 3.7 shows the brick image squared.

Once the brick image is squared, the offset filter should be applied. This will show how the seams will appear. The offset brick tiles are shown in Figure 3.7.

Figure 3.7: Bricks with Seams Exposed

Look at the seams. You can see that the colors of the bricks do not exactly match. There are also lines where the brick mortar lines up. The bandage tool is generally not helpful here. The bandage tool will damage the pattern of the bricks. The seam would be removed, but the image would no longer look quite like bricks.

The smudge tool is a good choice to fix this image. The smudge tool looks like a small finger pressing down. Use the smudge tool to even out the color differences and remove the brick lines. Figure 3.8 shows the bricks with the seams removed.

Figure 3.8: Bricks Without Seams

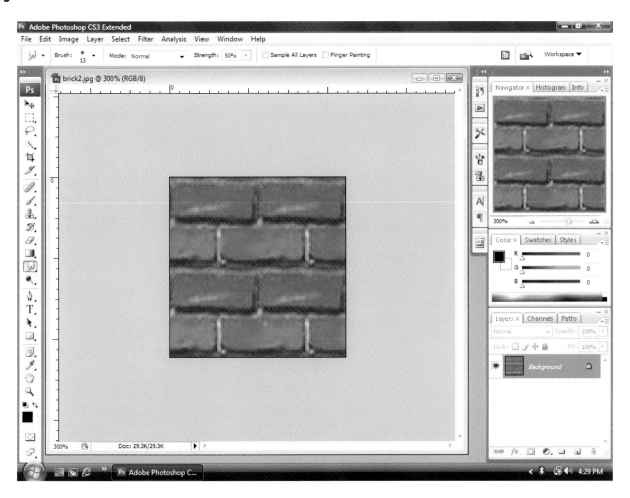

Now that the seams have been removed, the offset can be removed. As discussed in the previous section, the offset is removed by applying the exact same offset that was first applied. The two cancel each other out and the image returns to its regular state. The brick texture is now ready to be saved and uploaded to Second Life.

Using Tileable Textures in Second Life

When a texture is first selected in Second Life, there are no repeats. Therefore, a tileable texture will simply expand to the size of the prim. As a result, there will be only one tile, as shown in Figure 3.9.

Figure 3.9: Bricks With No Repeat

To select the repeats for a prim, right click and select "Edit" for the prim. Select the "Texture" tab. Here you will see "Repeats Per Face," which requires both horizontal and vertical values. For this example, a value of five was entered for both horizontal and vertical, as shown in Figure 3.10.

Figure 3.10: Setting a Repeat for the Bricks

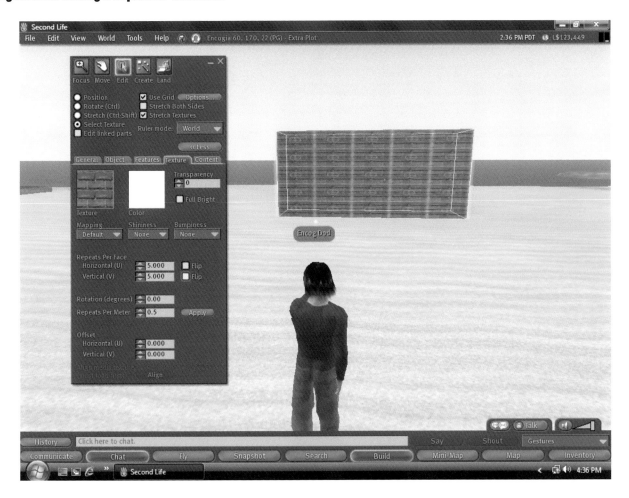

Once the repeat value has been changed, the image appears as shown in Figure 3.11.

Figure 3.11: Bricks With a Repeat

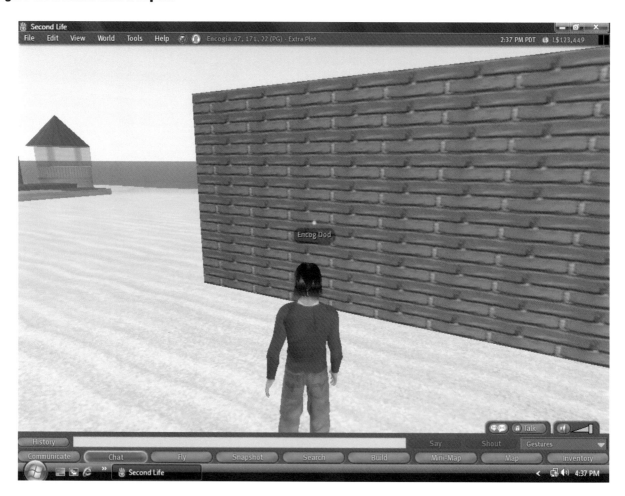

As you can see, the individual bricks are smaller, but they cover the entire prim.

Summary

Tileable textures are very useful in Second Life. A tileable texture is a texture that can be repeated over a prim in a grid type fashion. There should be no visible seams between the texture elements. To eliminate seams, special techniques can be employed using Photoshop.

Chapters 2 and 3 focused on using Adobe Photoshop as the image editor. However, Photoshop is not the only image editor that can be used with Second Life. The GNU Image Manipulation Program (GIMP) is a free image editor. The next chapter will explain how to use GIMP to perform many of the tasks explained in Chapters 2 and 3.

CHAPTER 4: USING GIMP

- Using GIMP in Place of Photoshop
- Cropping and Resizing Images With GIMP
- Creating Alpha Channels With GIMP
- Creating Tileable Textures With GIMP

So far, all image editing presented in this book has been accomplished using Adobe Photoshop. Adobe Photoshop is a commercial image editor. Photoshop is very powerful and is one of the most commonly used image editing programs. However, Photoshop is not the only way to edit images. The GNU Image Manipulation Program (GIMP) is an open source image editor that can be downloaded for free.

This chapter presents only a brief introduction into GIMP 2.2. The features of GIMP that are most commonly used for Second Life will be covered. For those interested in mastering GIMP, there are several books dedicated to the program. Additionally, this chapter only reviews how to perform operations already covered in Chapters 2 and 3. Chapters 2 and 3 should be reviewed prior to reading this chapter.

GIMP can be obtained from the following URL:

`http://www.gimp.org/`

Once downloaded, GIMP can be started from the "Windows Start" button. Figure 4.1 shows how the screen will appear when GIMP is first launched.

Figure 4.1: GIMP

As can be seen in Figure 4.1, GIMP is divided into three primary windows.

The first window, on the far left, is the tool palette. The tool palette window contains the menu bar for GIMP. The "File," "Edit," and other windows reside here. The tool palette is just below the menu bar. The tool palette contains all of the tools available in GIMP. Several of these tools will be introduced in this chapter.

The second window, in the middle, is the document window. The document window contains the document that is currently being edited. When a tool is selected from the tool palette, the tool will generally be used on the document window.

The third window, on the far right, holds additional palettes. There are several additional palettes, beyond the tool palette, that are provided by GIMP. These include the layers, channels, undo history, and path palettes. This chapter will explain the channel layer and how it can be used to create alpha channels for transparency.

Cropping and Resizing Images With GIMP

Cropping and resizing in GIMP is accomplished much as it is in Photoshop. GIMP provides methods for cropping, resizing an image, and resizing the canvas. These methods all perform the same fundamental operations as in Photoshop. The following sections will describe how these can be accomplished.

Cropping in GIMP

Cropping in GIMP is accomplished as it is in Photoshop. For example, assume that the Ferris wheel shown in Figure 4.1 is the only part of the image desired. The picture would be cropped to include only the Ferris wheel. To do this, you must select the "Select Rectangular Regions" tool from the tools palette. It looks like a dotted rectangle.

Draw a rectangle around the Ferris wheel. Once the rectangle encloses the Ferris wheel, select "Crop" from the "Crop Image" menu.

Changing the Image Size in GIMP

The image size can also be adjusted in GIMP as it is in Photoshop. This is done by selecting "Scale Image" from the "Image" menu. Selecting this option will bring up the Scale Image Window, as shown in Figure 4.2.

Figure 4.2: Scale Image

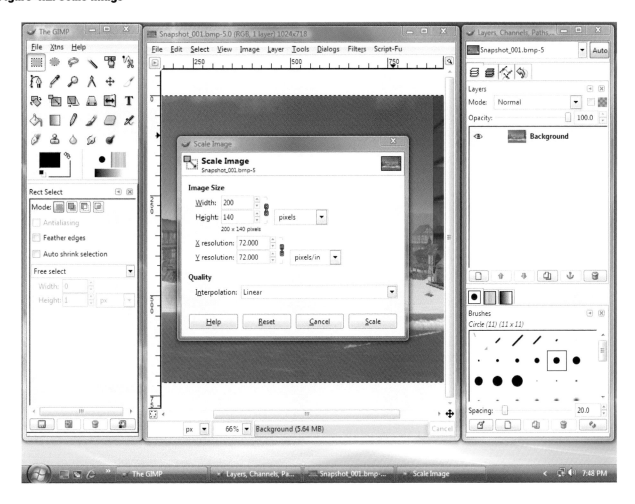

From this window, the height and width of the image can be adjusted. By default, the height and width are constrained, so the aspect ratio of the image cannot change. This prevents the image from stretching. Entering a value for the width will force a new height value to be calculated. This height value will simply change the size of the image and not stretch it. The same calculation will be performed on the width, if a new value is entered for the height. To change the height and width independently, and potentially stretch the image, click the small chain-link icon between the width and height.

For this example, the image will be resized to a width of 200 and a height of 140. Once this resizing is done, the image will appear as shown in Figure 4.3.

Figure 4.3: The Amusement Park Resized

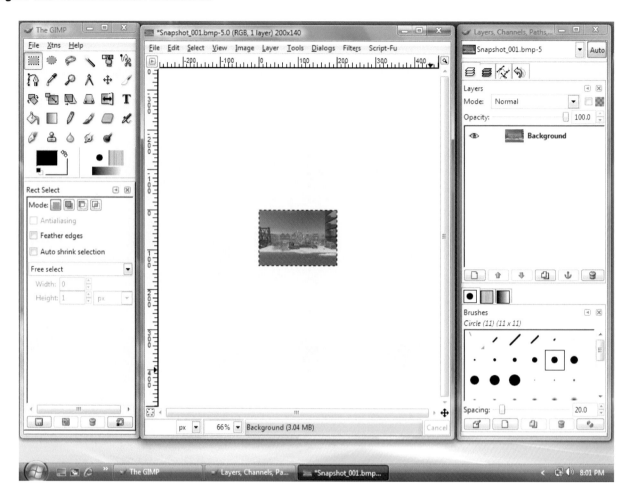

As can be seen in Figure 4.3, no part of the image was dropped. The image is not much smaller, but the resolution is much lower.

Changing the Canvas Size in GIMP

Just as with Photoshop, changing the canvas size in GIMP could result in part of an image being discarded. To change the canvas size, choose "Canvas Size" from the "Image" menu. The window shown in Figure 4.4 will be displayed.

Figure 4.4: Change Canvas Size

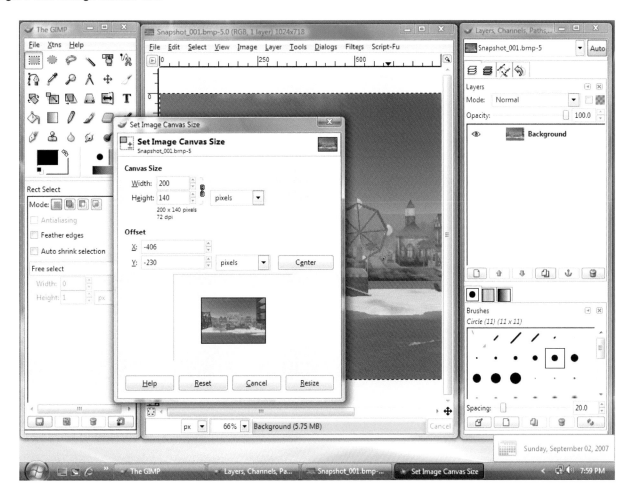

Changing the canvas size is accomplished somewhat differently in GIMP than in Photoshop. As in Photoshop, the height and width are specified. For this example, a height of 140 and a width of 200 are chosen. While Photoshop used a grid of 12 squares to communicate which part of the image should be discarded, GIMP uses offsets. As can be seen in Figure 4.4, a small square is provided to choose which part of the image to keep. In Figure 4.4, this rectangle is placed on the top part of the Ferris wheel. When the canvas is resized, this is what will remain. Figure 4.5 shows the resized canvas.

Figure 4.5: The Resized Canvas

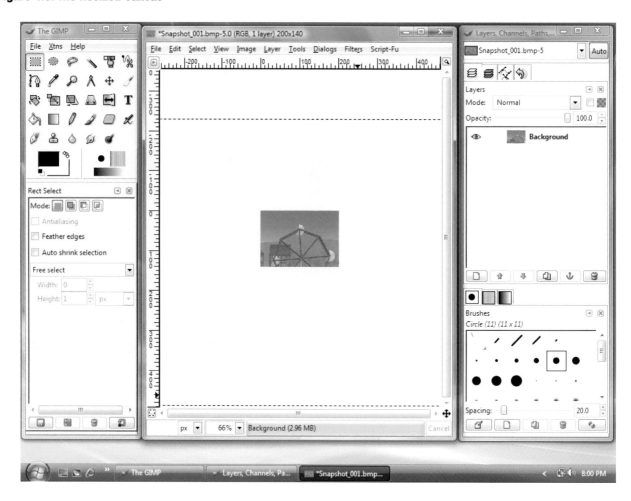

Both of the operations illustrated in Figures 4.3 and 4.5 changed the size of the image to 200 x 140. However the end results were quite different. Figures 4.3 and 4.5 illustrate the difference between changing the image size and changing the canvas size.

Creating Alpha Channels With GIMP

The fundamental concept of an alpha channel is the same in GIMP as it is in Photoshop. The alpha channel is a fourth channel, in addition to the red, green, and blue values, which specifies the transparency of an image. However, while the concept is the same, the method used to create an alpha channel is very different from the method used in Photoshop.

The first step is to open an image that is to be made transparent. The same window texture that was used in Chapter 3 will be used for this example. Once the image is open, choose "Transparency" from the "Layer" menu. Then choose "Add Alpha Channel" from the "Transparency" menu. This will add an alpha channel to the image. The alpha channel can be seen by clicking the "Channels" tab on the "Layers, Channels, Paths" window. Now that the alpha channel has been created, each windowpane must be selected, one-by-one, and added to the alpha channel. Once the first pane is selected, select "Clear" on the "Edit" menu. Repeat this process for all 12 windowpanes. Once all of the panes have been cleared, the image should look like Figure 4.6.

Figure 4.6: A Transparent Window

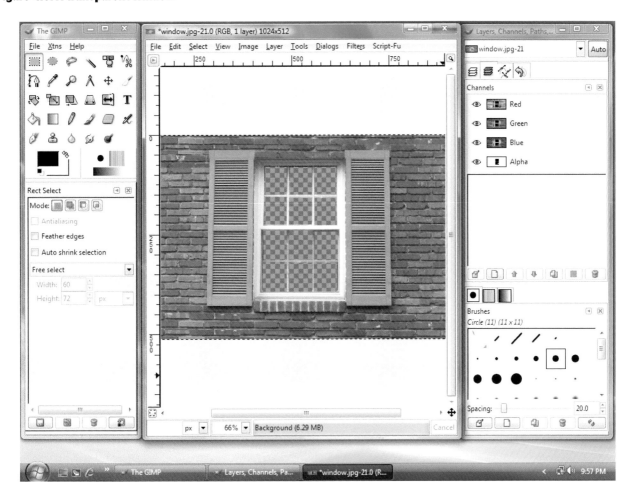

The window should now be saved as a Targa file. This is done by selecting "Save As" from the "File" menu. Simply save the image as a file with the extension of TGA. GIMP will save the file in its Targa format.

Creating Tileable Textures With GIMP

GIMP makes it very easy to create tileable textures. The procedure for creating a tileable texture in GIMP is almost the same as in Photoshop. Just as in Photoshop, the first step is to use a tool to offset the image. This will show where the seams are. Then, using several other GIMP tools, the seams should be "smoothed out" so they are no longer visible.

Begin by opening the image that is to be made tileable. The same brick texture that was used in Chapter 3 will be used for this example. The image should now be offset. To do this, select "Transform" from the "Layer" menu. Then, select "Offset" from the "Transform" submenu. The display will appear as shown in Figure 4.7.

Figure 4.7: Offset a Layer

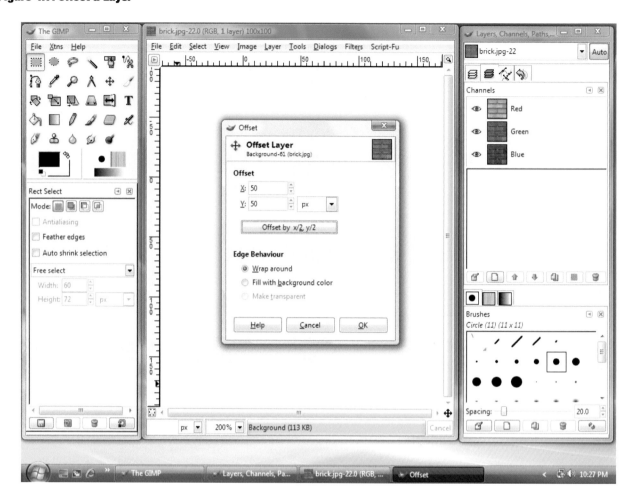

Begin by clicking the "Offset by x/2, y/2." Then click "OK." The figure appears as shown in Figure 4.8. The seams are clearly visible.

Figure 4.8: Brick Texture Offset

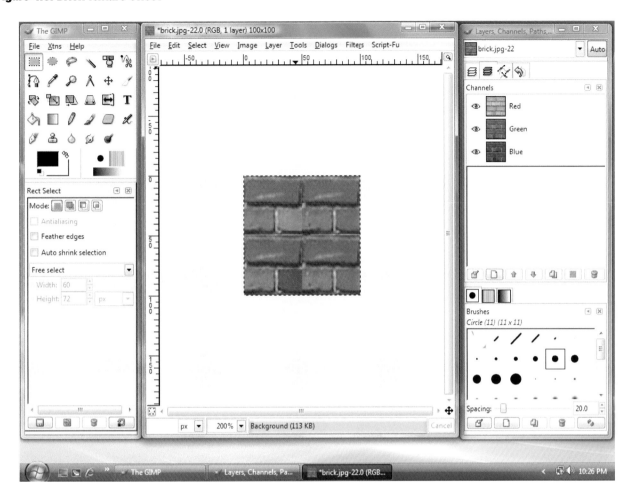

Now that the seams are clearly visible, they should be removed. The main tools used in GIMP to remove seams are the "Rubber Stamp," "Blur or Sharpen," and the "Smudge" tools. It is best to try out each tool to see what effect it has.

Once the seams have been fixed, the "Offset" window should be used again to undo the offset. Just as with Photoshop, the method to undo the offset is to apply the same "Offset Transformation."

Summary

Prior to this chapter, all editing of graphics was accomplished using Adobe Photoshop. The GNU Image Manipulation Program (GIMP) can also be used to perform image editing. GIMP provides many of the same functions offered by Photoshop. GIMP is an open source image editor that can be freely downloaded.

Animations are a very important part of Second Life. Animations allow the avatars to perform a sequence of moves. Animations are created outside Second Life and then uploaded. The next chapter will introduce animations.

CHAPTER 5: CREATING ANIMATIONS

- Understanding Animations
- Using Avimator
- Creating a Static Pose
- Creating Multiframe Animations
- Uploading Animations to Second Life

Animations allow avatars to move their arms, legs, and other body parts in ways that mimic actual human movement. Anything that causes an avatar to move a body part is considered an animation. Second Life has many built-in animations. Common avatar actions, such as walking, running, flying, sitting, and standing up, can all be accomplished using built-in animations.

The Second Life client does not automatically use all built-in animations. There are many built-in animations that are never used unless a developer specifically includes them in a script or the user chooses to specifically invoke them. These animations allow avatars to perform movements such as dance, hold a gun, hold a sword, and other frequently desired actions. The complete list of built-in animations is presented in Table 5.1.

Before creating an animation, the built-in animations should be checked. There may already be an animation that meets your requirements. If there is no built-in animation that meets your requirements, then a new animation must be created. Second Life requires animations to be uploaded in much the same way textures are uploaded. Second Life stores animations in the Biovision Hierarchy (BVH) file format. The BVH format is nothing more than a non-XML hierarchical file format that specifies the angles between the joints of an avatar's body parts.

While it is possible to create a BVH file by hand using a text editor, most BVH files are created using a third-party program, such as Avimator.

Table 5.1: Second Life Built-In Animations

aim_l_bow	express_afraid_emote	express_wink_emote	no_unhappy	soft_land
aim_r_bazooka	express_anger	express_worry	nyanya	stand
aim_r_handgun	express_anger_emote	express_worry_emote	peace	stand_1
aim_r_rifle	express_bored	falldown	point_me	stand_2
angry_fingerwag	express_bored_emote	female_walk	point_you	stand_3
angry_tantrum	express_cry	fist_pump	prejump	stand_4
away	express_cry_emote	fly	punch_l	standup
backflip	express_disdain	flyslow	punch_onetwo	stretch
blowkiss	express_embarrassed	hello	punch_r	stride
bow	express_embarrassed_emote	hold_l_bow	rps_countdown	surf
brush	express_frown	hold_r_bazooka	rps_paper	sword_strike_r
busy	express_kiss	hold_r_handgun	rps_rock	talk
clap	express_laugh	hold_r_rifle	rps_scissors	throw_r
courtbow	express_laugh_emote	hold_throw_r	run	tryon_shirt
crouch	express_open_mouth	hover	salute	turn_180
crouchwalk	express_repulsed	hover_down	shoot_l_bow	turnback_180
dance1	express_repulsed_emote	hover_up	shout	turnleft
dance2	express_sad	impatient	sit	turnright
dance3	express_sad_emote	jump	sit_female	type
dance4	express_shrug	jumpforjoy	sit_generic	walk
dance5	express_shrug_emote	kick_roundhouse_r	sit_ground	whisper
dance6	express_smile	kissmybutt	sit_to_stand	whistle
dance7	express_surprise	land	sleep	wink_hollywood
dance8	express_surprise_emote	laugh_short	smoke_idle	yes_happy
dead	express_tongue_out	motorcycle_sit	smoke_inhale	yes_head
drink	express_toothsmile	musclebeach	smoke_throw_down	yoga_float
express_afraid	express_wink	no_head	snapshot	

Using Avimator

Avimator is a free, open-source avatar animation tool developed for use with Second Life. The animations used in this book will be created with Avimator 0.4. Avimator can be downloaded from the following URL:

`http://www.avimator.com/`

When Avimator is first launched, the main screen is displayed, as shown in Figure 5.1.

Figure 5.1: Avimator

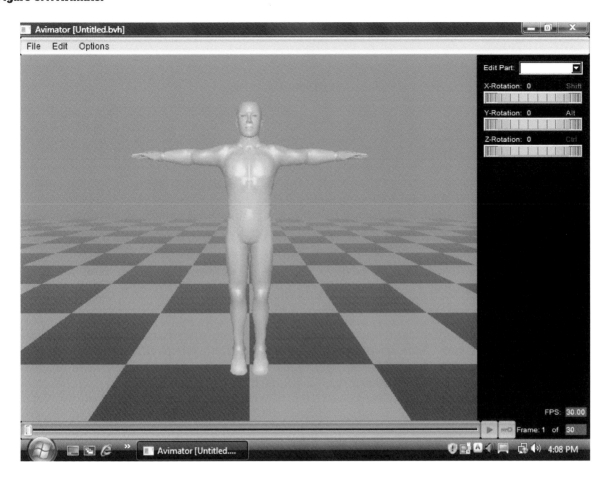

As can be seen in Figure 5.1, Avimator opens with a male avatar standing in the center of the screen. If a female avatar is preferred, select "Female" from the "Options" menu.

An animation is a collection of frames. To create an animation, the avatar is moved into position for each of the different frames. Toward the bottom of Figure 5.1, a set of sample frames is shown. Clicking the green "Play" button will take the avatar through the animated sequence. To edit an individual frame, click and drag the yellow frame selector to the correct frame. By default, 30 frames are provided. If a different number of frames is needed, enter the desired value at the bottom of the screen where it says "Frame: 1 of 30." Simply change the number 30 to the desired number of frames. Most values shown on the Avimator window can be changed in this way. A number can either be entered directly, or changed using one of the sliders.

While editing the animation, it may be necessary to view the avatar from different angles. You can change the camera's perspective by clicking the mouse and dragging. To zoom in and out, use the scroll wheel on the mouse.

There are two types of animations that you can create:

• Poses
• Multiframe Animations

A pose simply sets the avatar in a particular position. Once the avatar has assumed this position, no further movement will occur. Multiframe animations cycle the avatar through a series of poses. This makes it appear as though the avatar is moving.

Understanding Frames

Before creating poses or multiframe animated sequences, it is important to understand the different types of frames that make up an Avimator animation file and how they are used. There are a total of three different frame types used by Avimator:

- Reference Frames
- Key Frames
- Regular Frames

The first frame in an Avimator animation file is called the reference frame. The reference frame should have all joints set to zero rotation. Second Life compares subsequent frames to the reference frame to determine what has changed. A reference frame will therefore have the avatar standing in a t-shaped configuration, as shown in Figure 5.1.

The reference frame allows for the creation of an animation that only moves part of an avatar. For example, if the desire is to create an animation that will make the avatar wave his right arm, only the joint settings for the right arm would be changed. The remainder of the settings would stay the same as those specified in the reference frame. Therefore, only the right arm would move. This is important, because more than one animation can be running at a time. An animation that affects the left arm can be running simultaneously with an animation that moves the right arm.

Key frames are the frames in which animations actually occur. Key frames are selected by clicking the "key" button near the bottom of the Avimator screen. Any frame in which the avatar has been altered should be registered as a key frame. Second Life will approximate to determine the number of frames to be displayed between the key frames. As long as the key frames are close enough together, it is unnecessary to animate every intermediate frame between two key frames.

Regular frames are all of the frames that are not reference or key frames. They do not contribute to the animation, as only the key frames are displayed. However, they act as useful placeholders. If an animation is specified which displays 30 frames per second, and needs to last 3 seconds, a total of 90 frames would be required. However, it is not necessary to animate each of the 90 individual frames. Rather, every tenth frame might be animated. Each of these animated frames is a key frame, and the frames between them are regular frames.

It can be somewhat tricky to determine whether or not a frame is a key frame. Generally, if a frame is a key frame, the key symbol will be present at the bottom of the page. Additionally, the avatar will turn light green. Figure 5.2 shows a key frame.

Figure 5.2: A Key Frame

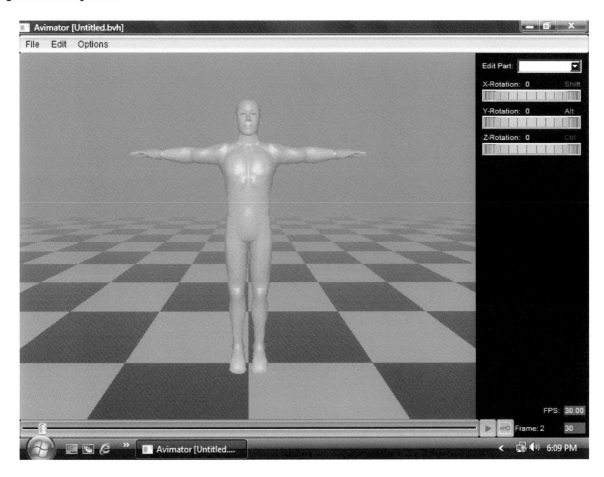

However, this is not always the case. If an animation has only two frames, then the avatar will not be displayed in light green in either frame. Additionally, both frames will have the key symbol, even though the first frame is the reference frame, and the second is a key frame.

Understanding Joints

Each frame is basically a set of rotations. There is one rotation per joint. Following is a list of all the joints, as contained in the drop list near the top right side of the Avimator screen:

- abdomen
- chest
- head
- hip
- lCollar
- lFoot
- lForeArm
- lHand
- lShin
- lShldr
- lThigh
- neck
- rCollar
- rFoot
- rForeArm
- rHand
- rShin
- rShldr
- rThigh

Not all joints are created equal. The hip joint has special features, which will be discussed in a moment. The x, y, and z rotations can be edited for any joint, except the hip. These three variables are the only variables that affect the joints. They can be seen in Figure 5.1.

The hip joint has additional variables. The additional variables are displayed for editing when the hip joint is selected. These variables can be seen in Figure 5.3.

Figure 5.3: Adjusting the Position of the Hip

The hip also has an x, y, and z position. Why is a position needed? Consider if the avatar were moved to a position where he was sitting on the ground. If the hip position were not adjusted, the avatar would not be sitting on the ground, it would be floating above the ground! By adjusting the z position of the hip, the avatar can be placed on the ground. The position of the hip defines the position of the avatar.

The angle of the hip is also very important, since it has a global effect on an avatar. The hip angle defines the angle of the entire avatar. By adjusting the hip angle, an avatar can be made to lie on his back or stand on his head.

Creating a Static Pose

To create a pose, enter a value of two for the number of frames. While it may seem illogical to specify two frames for creating a pose that by definition is a single position, remember from the previous section that the first frame is always the reference frame. The second frame in the animation file will be the single key frame.

Move to the key frame, which is the second frame. Next, select the first body part to be positioned. There are two ways to select a body part. The first is to simply click on the body part. The selected body part will be highlighted and red, green, and blue rotational axes will be displayed around the part. Alternatively, body parts can be selected using the pull-down menu.

Once the body part has been selected, it can be rotated. There are three different ways to rotate a body part:

- While holding down "Shift," "Ctrl," or "Alt," click and drag the body part.
- Enter values for the x, y, and z rotation.
- Click and drag the sliders beneath the x, y, and z rotation.

It is also possible to shift-click and select more than one body part at once. This allows multiple body parts to be rotated at the same time.

For this animation example, we will create an avatar with his left hand held out in a "stop" position. First, create an animation with two frames. Move to the second frame. Next, select the lShldr joint and rotate it to 90 degrees. Now, select the lHand joint and rotate the hand to 80 degrees. The avatar should now appear as in Figure 5.4.

Figure 5.4: Avatar in the STOP Position

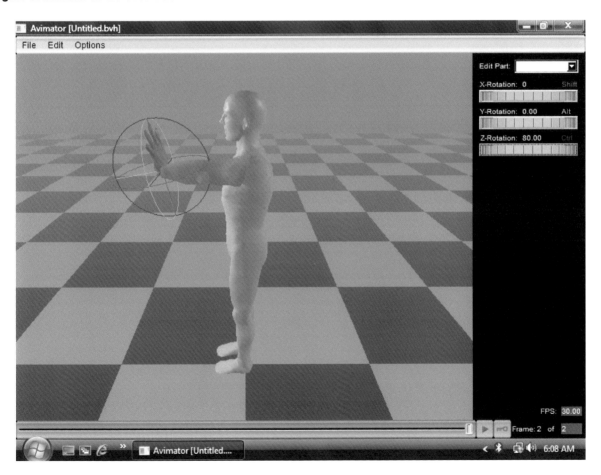

Notice how the hand cannot be rotated to 90 degrees? Why is that? Does your own hand rotate to 90 degrees without assistance? Avimator is programmed to only allow rotation of the joints to angles that are possible, without injury, for humans to achieve. However, these constraints can be disabled. Select the "Options" menu and then select "Joint Limits." This can be used to toggle the joint limits on and off.

The pose is now created and can be saved to a file, such as "stop.bvh". This is done by selecting a save option from the "File" menu. Once saved, the pose is ready to be uploaded. Uploading a BVH file to Second Life will be covered later in this chapter.

Creating Multiframe Animations

In the last section, a single pose was created. Animations can also be created. An animation is a series of poses that are played in succession. Animations can either be looped or non-looped. A looped animation will continue to play repeatedly. A non-looped animation will play only once.

The example animation for this chapter will show an avatar waving goodbye. This will be a looped animation. The first step is to plan the animation. There will be a total of four key frames, as shown in Figure 5.5.

Figure 5.5: Wave Key Frames

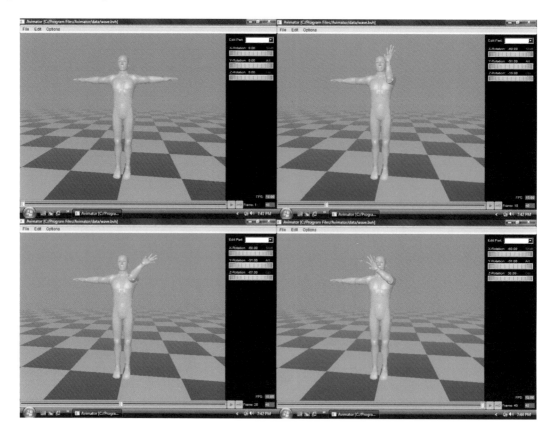

The above figure shows frames numbered 1, 10, 20, and 40. One important note, frames 2 and 40 are nearly identical. It is always important when looping to end the animation with the avatar in the same position he started in. If this is not done, the avatar will "skip" between the first and last frames.

Uploading Animations to Second Life

Once an animation has been saved to a BVH file, it can be uploaded to Second Life. To upload an animation, choose "Upload Animation" from the "File" menu. Figure 5.6 shows the upload dialog box for an animation.

Figure 5.6: Uploading an Animation to Second Life

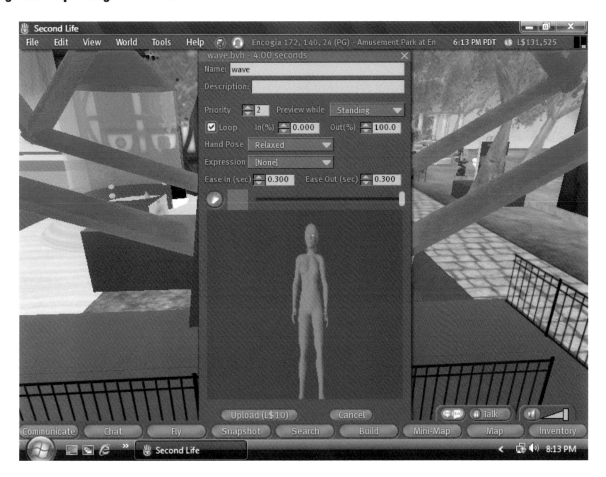

The priority number specifies the priority for this animation relative to the priorities of other animations that may want to move the same body parts this animation moves. Several animations can be used at once, if they use different body parts. However, if two animations try to use the same body part, then the priority number is used to determine which animation will be used to move the part.

The loop checkbox should be checked for both a pose and a multiframe animation that should loop. The only time the loop checkbox should not be checked is when the multiframe animation does not loop. The beginning and ending frames are specified using "In%" and "Out%." Normally, these values are set to zero and 100, respectively, to play the entire animation.

The hand pose option allows one of several different hand poses to be selected. The expression option allows a facial expression to be selected. The "ease in" and "ease out" options specify how much time the avatar takes to ease into and out of the animation. Ease in can be useful for instructing the avatar to take more or less time to complete the first animation loop. Ease out is not used with a looping animation.

Once the animation has been uploaded, it is added to the animations in your inventory. Double click the animation to play it in the Second Life world. Figure 5.7 shows the wave animation being played in Second Life.

Figure 5.7: Wave Animation in Second Life

The animation can now be used with any script that makes use of animations.

Summary

Animations have many uses in Second Life. Animations can be played directly from the inventory to cause an avatar to perform actions anywhere in Second Life. Animations are also commonly embedded into objects and accessed by scripts.

Animations must be created in a program external to Second Life. This chapter explained how to create animations using Avimator. Avimator is a free, open-source program that creates the BVH files that Second Life requires for animations. Animations are made up of a series of frames. The first frame, or reference frame, specifies what body parts are moved to create the animation. Key frames are those frames that contain the stages of the animation. The regular frames are automatically generated by Second Life to fill in the space between the key frames.

Audio can be recorded and played in Second Life. Audio files can be played directly by users or used in conjunction with scripts. The next chapter will explain how to record and edit audio files for Second Life.

CHAPTER 6: COMPOSING AUDIO FILES

- Second Life Audio Requirements
- Downloading Audio Files
- Using Audacity
- Recording Audio
- Uploading Audio to Second Life

Second Life allows audio files to be uploaded. These audio files can then be played in the Second Life world. Audio files are added by selecting "Upload Sound (L$10)" from the file menu. It costs 10 Linden dollars to upload an audio file, which is equivalent to about five cents (USD).

Second Life has very specific requirements regarding the types of audio files that can be uploaded. An audio file may only be used in Second Life if it meets the following criteria:

- Must be in Microsoft WAV (.wav) format
- Must have a sample rate of 44,100 hertz
- Must be less than 10 seconds in playtime

Many audio files found on the Internet will not meet these criteria. Fortunately, it is relatively easy to change an audio file into the format needed by Second Life using a program such as Audacity. Audacity will be covered in greater detail later in this chapter.

There are two primary means of obtaining audio files for Second Life:

- Downloading audio from the Internet
- Recording audio

Downloading Audio Files

There are many sources for audio files on the Internet. Not all audio files found on the Internet can be legally used within Second Life. Some audio files are copyrighted. Always check the source of an audio file to determine the legality of using it. Whenever in doubt, consult an attorney. Determining the legal status of an audio file found on the Internet is beyond the scope of this book.

Internet File Formats

Audio files are available on the Internet in many different formats. Table 6.1 summarizes the formats available.

Table 6.1: Common Internet Audio Formats

Sound Format	Description
AIFF	Audio Interchange File Format (AIFF) is a file format commonly used on UNIX computer systems. It is similar to WAV, in that shorter audio clips are often stored as AIFF files. AIFF uses the file extension .aiff.
MP3	MP3 is a very popular audio format for songs. There are many illegally recorded MP3s of commercial songs available on the Internet. MP3s will almost always be over the 10-second limit imposed by Second Life. In such cases, a program such as Audacity is required to create a 10-second "clip" of some portion of the song. MP3 uses the file extension .mp3.
OGG/Vorbis	OGG/Vorbis, like MP3 is generally used to record longer audio files, such as songs. OGG/Vorbis was created to be an open-source alternative to MP3. OGG/Vorbis uses the file extension .ogg.
WAV	WAV is the standard format for the Microsoft Windows operating systems. WAV files are stored with the .wav file extension, and are very common on the Internet. WAV files are more commonly used for short audio clips than full-length songs. If stored with the correct frequency, WAV files can be directly uploaded to Second Life. WAV uses the file extension .wav.

A program such as Audacity can easily convert between the various file formats, so it is not necessary to limit your selection of audio files based on their format.

Finding Audio Files to Download

A search engine is the best way to start searching for audio files. The Google search engine will be used for the examples in this book. Other search engines, such as Yahoo, could also be used. The Google search engine can be found at the following address:

```
http://www.google.com
```

As an example, suppose you need the sound of a train. It is usually best to search for the term needed along with the sound format desired. For example, to search for train sounds, the following search term could be used.

```
train wav
```

If the above search term were submitted to Google, the results shown in Figure 6.1 would be returned.

Figure 6.1: Searching Google for Sounds

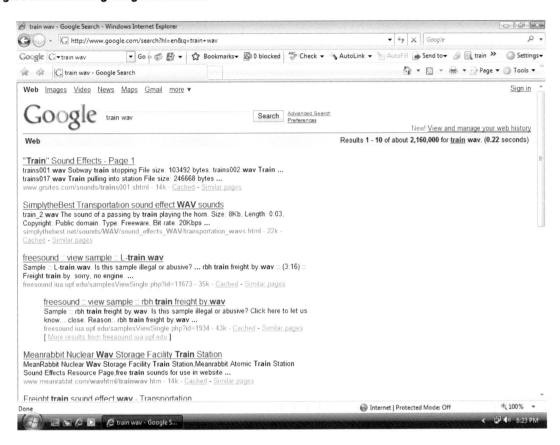

As can be seen from the above list, several train sounds have been located. Simply click the link desired and download the appropriate sound.

Using Audacity

There are many different programs that can be used to record and edit audio. Some are free, and some are commercial and require payment. This book will make use of a sound editor called Audacity. Audacity is a free, easy-to-use audio editor and recorder for Windows, Mac OS X, GNU/Linux, and other operating systems. Audacity can be used to:

- Record live audio.
- Convert tapes and records into digital recordings or CDs.
- Edit OGG/Vorbis, MP3, and WAV sound files.
- Cut, copy, splice, and mix sounds together.
- Change the speed or pitch of a recording.

Audacity can be downloaded from the following URL:

`http://audacity.sourceforge.net/`

This book uses Audacity 1.3. When you launch audacity, the main screen will be displayed, as shown in Figure 6.2.

Figure 6.2: Audacity

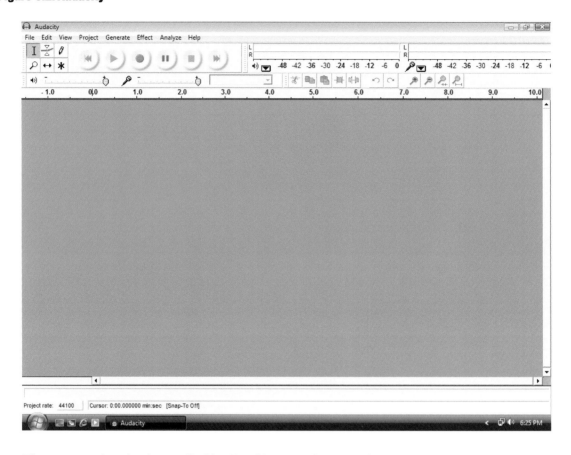

The next step is to load an audio file. For this example one of the train sounds found earlier will be opened. This file is named train3.wav. It is not necessary to use this exact file. Any audio file will do. Once train3.wav has been opened, you will see a screen similar to the one shown in Figure 6.3.

Figure 6.3: Audacity With a Sound Loaded

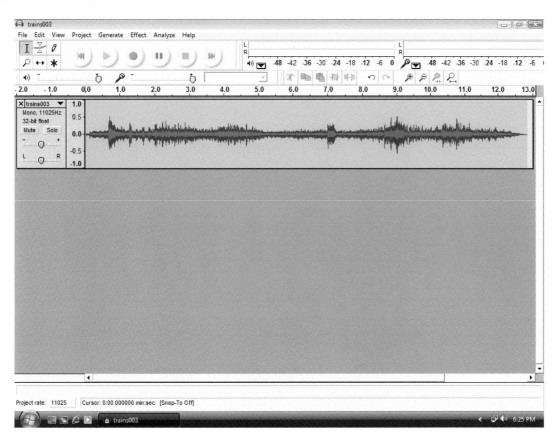

The blue wave in the middle of the screen represents the sound that is being edited. By examining Figure 6.3, several things are immediately apparent about the sound. First, the sound is too long for Second Life. Notice the numbers just above the blue wave. These numbers represent seconds. The sound stops at 13, indicating the sound is 13 seconds long.

Additionally, notice the "Project Rate." This number can be seen at the bottom left corner of the screen. This is the frequency at which the sound was recorded. The sound seen in Figure 6.3 was recorded at 11,025 hertz. As mentioned earlier in this chapter, all Second Life audio must be recorded at 44,100 hertz. Therefore, before this sound can be used in Second Life, several things must happen:

- The sound must be trimmed to less than 10 seconds
- The sound must be adjusted to 44,100 hertz
- The new sound must be saved as a .wav file

These three steps are very common in preparing sound for Second Life. They will need to be performed on many of the sounds downloaded from the Internet, to prepare the files to meet Second Life's audio requirements. The next section covers how to trim sounds to less than 10 seconds.

Trimming the Sound

When a sound is trimmed to less than 10 seconds, part of the sound must be discarded. To trim a sound, the desired portion of the sound, shown by the blue wave, is selected by dragging the mouse.

While the blue wave gives some indication of the underlying sound, it is hard to tell exactly what is being trimmed simply by looking at the blue wave. If the green "Play" button is clicked, the sound will play. A line will passes over the blue wave as the sound plays. This line indicates which part of the blue wave is actually being played.

The part of the blue wave that should be kept can be selected by dragging the mouse. Figure 6.4 shows the sound with part of the blue wave selected.

Figure 6.4: Selecting the Part of the Sound to Keep

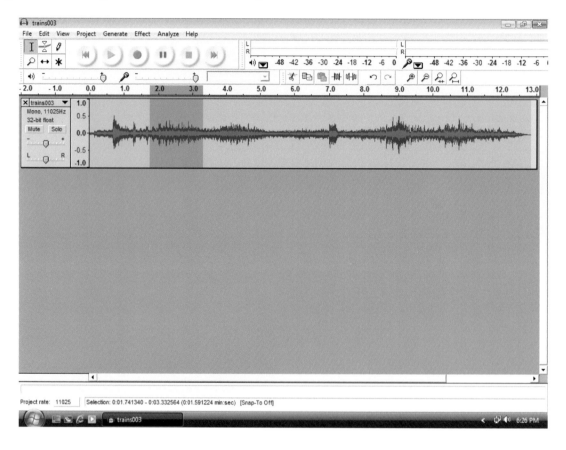

To verify that the correct region has been selected, click the "Play" button. Now only the selected region of the sound wave will play. Once the desired region has been identified, "Copy" should be selected from the "Edit" menu. Doing so will cause the selected part of the sound wave to be copied to the clipboard.

Now create a new sound file by clicking "New" on the "File" menu. This will create a new sound file. The clipboard should now be pasted into this file by selecting the "Paste" option of the "Edit" menu.

Changing the Sample Rate

When the sound was pasted into the new sound file, the sample rate was also changed to 44,100 hertz. This automatically brought the sound to the correct sample rate for Second Life. No further adjustments to the frequency are needed. The current sample rate can be verified by looking at the number at the bottom left of the screen. This number must be 44,100 for Second Life.

If the sample rate did need to be changed, it would easy to accomplish. Simply click the number at the bottom left of the screen. A small pop-up window would appear. This pop-up can be used to choose the correct sample rate.

Saving a WAV File

The sound has now been properly transformed. It has the correct sample rate and is under 10 seconds. It should now be saved as a Microsoft WAV file. To do this, select "Export As WAV" from the "File" menu. The window shown in Figure 6.5 will be displayed.

Figure 6.5: Export as WAV

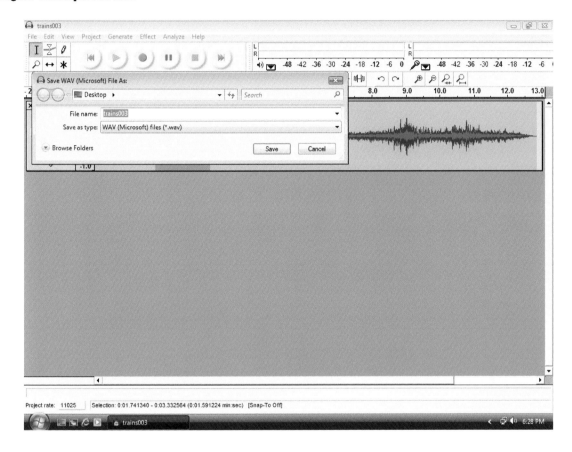

Simply select a file name and save the audio. The sound file is now ready to be uploaded to Second Life. Uploading a file to Second Life is covered later in this Chapter.

Other Useful Audio Transformations

There are other transformations that Audacity can perform on audio files. Most of these are listed in the "Effects" menu. There are quite a few such effects. The best way to become familiar with each is to experiment with them.

Some of the more useful effects are:

- Amplify
- Click Removal
- Echo
- Fade In
- Fade Out
- Noise Removal

There are times when a sound file is too quiet. In such cases, the amplify effect can be used to increase the volume of the sound. Other effects can be used to create special effects. For example, the Echo effect can be used to simulate an echo inside a cave.

Looping Sound

Often, a sound needs to be looped. A looped sound plays repeatedly. It is therefore important that the sound at the end of the clip flows smoothly with the sound at the beginning of the clip. This is accomplished by selecting a portion of the sound where the pitch and volume are constant.

Audacity provides the ability to play a selected region in a loop, so you can hear it before saving it to a file. In order to do so, select the part of the sound wave that looks like a good candidate for a loop. Then, hold down the "Shift" key while clicking the green "Play" button. This will cause the sound to be played in a loop. If a skip is heard when it repeats, the region selected was not a good choice for the loop. Select a new area and repeat the process.

Recording Audio

It is also possible to use Audacity to record audio from the real world for use in Second Life. To do this, press the red "Record" button. The microphone will be activated and Audacity will record the input. The recording process is shown in Figure 6.6.

Figure 6.6: Recording a Sound

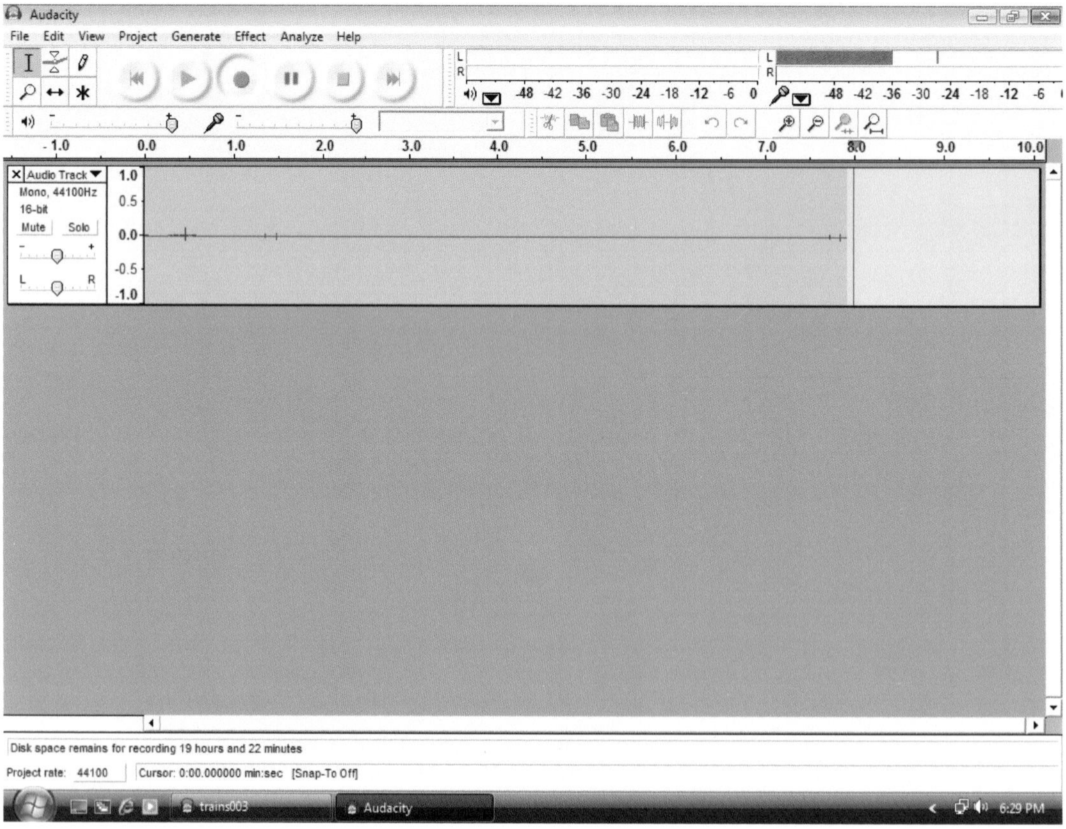

The recording will continue until the yellow "Stop" button is clicked.

A laptop can be useful for recording audio. A laptop allows the recording to be done near where the "sound" actually occurs. For example, I recorded the sound of my car's engine to provide the sound for a car that I had created in Second Life. To do this, I took my laptop to the car, since it was not possible to take my car to the desktop!

I used a microphone with a long cord. The microphone was draped from the passenger's seat to under the hood of the car. This was the location that allowed for the clearest recording of the car starting and running. Using the laptop's built-in microphone did not produce a very clean recording of the engine's sounds.

Often, unwanted whitespace will be recorded either before or after the desired sound. Using the trimming techniques discussed earlier, extra whitespace can easily be removed.

Uploading Audio to Second Life

Once the final WAV file has been saved, it can be uploaded to Second Life. This is done by selecting "Upload Sound (L$10)" from the "File" menu. Once the sound has been uploaded, it will appear in the "sounds" folder of the inventory. Double click on the sound to play it.

Summary

This chapter introduced techniques which can be used to add sound to Second Life. Audacity, a free, third-party program can be used to edit sounds. Sounds can be trimmed to remove whitespace or to shorten them so they meet Second Life's 10-second maximum length requirement.

Second life has additional requirements for uploading sounds. All sounds must be in Microsoft WAV format, and must be recorded at 44,100 Hertz. Sounds found on the Internet can be converted to the proper format for Second Life using Audacity.

CHAPTER 7: SCULPTING PRIMS

- Understanding Sculpties
- Sculptypaint Basics
- From Sculptypaint to Second Life

Second Life introduced a new prim type in 2007 called a sculptured prim, or sculpty. Sculpties are different from other prim types in that a sculpty has no defined shape. A sculpty's shape is determined by a special texture. This texture is usually created using a 3D modeling program. There are many 3D modeling programs that can be used with Second Life. A few of them are listed here:

- Maya (`http://www.autodesk.com/maya`)
- Blender (`http://www.blender.org/`)
- Wings 3D (`http://www.wings3d.com/`)
- Sculptypaint (`http://www.xs4all.nl/~elout/sculptpaint/`)
- Rokuro and Tokoroten (`http://www.kanae.net/secondlife/`)

Maya is the only commercial modeler listed. It is one of the most advanced modeling software programs on the market and is used extensively by video game designers and movie professionals. Maya is expensive and has a steep learning curve. All of the other modelers in the list can be obtained free of charge from their respective web sites.

Blender is considered by many to be the most advanced open-source modeling program. Blender is capable of creating files that can be converted for use in Second Life. To convert Blender files, use the **prim.blender** found at the following URL:

`http://sourceforge.net/projects/primdotblender`

Wings 3D is another open-source modeling tool. Wings 3D offers far fewer capabilities than Blender, however almost all of the advanced features offered by Blender are not compatible with Second Life anyway. In addition, Second Life sculpties only support a mesh size of up to 64 x 63. Both Blender and Wings 3D allow far more complex models than Second Life will support. Like Blender, Wings 3D requires a special program to convert files from the Wings 3D format to a format that Second Life can use. A Second Life Wings 3D conversion plugin can be found at the following URL:

`http://wiki.secondlife.com/wiki/Wings 3D Exporter`

Maya, Blender, and Wings 3D are all generic modeling tools that were developed prior to the advent of Second Life. There are entire books written on Maya and Blender. To completely cover the use of either program would be beyond the scope of this book. Wings 3D has a much shallower learning curve than both Maya and Blender. Thus, Wings 3D is one of the most popular modeling tools used by Second Life members.

With the growing popularity of Second Life, there are now several modeling programs available which are specifically targeted at creating for the Second Life world. When you use a Second Life specific modeler, you don't have to worry about using features that are not supported by Second Life. Sculptypaint, Rokuro, and Tokoroten are examples of Second Life specific modelers. All three modelers have shallow learning curves. Sculptypaint is arguably the most advanced. Because of the introductory nature of this book, Sculptypaint will be discussed.

It should be noted that all three programs, Sculptypaint, Rokuro, and Tokoroten are less than a year old. Changes may occur in these immature programs that may invalidate some of the information in this book. Always check this book's errata page at the Heaton Research Website (`http://www.heatonresearch.com`) to make sure the material presented here has not been updated.

Sculptypaint Basics

Sculptypaint has a very basic user interface. This book uses Sculptypaint 0.9. It is somewhat different than standard Windows or Macintosh applications and can lead to some confusion. The main Sculptypaint screen, as shown in Figure 7.1, is displayed when the application is launched.

Figure 7.1: Sculptypaint

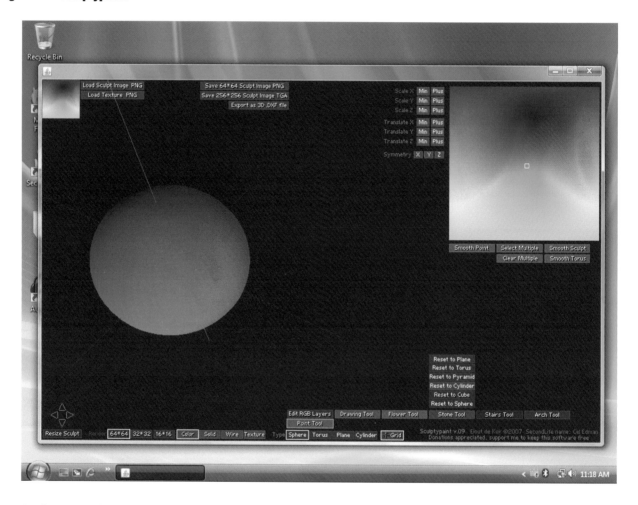

Sculptypaint shows the 3D object that is currently being designed. This object always starts off as a sphere. Think of this sphere as a lump of clay that can be molded into a desired shape. At the top left region of the window is the sculptured texture. This is the texture that will be sent to Second Life to create the sculpty. Seeing the image in this form is of little value, however Sculptypaint still displays it.

Near the top of the window are various options for loading and saving textures. The sculpty can also be exported as a DXF file. This allows the sculpty to be read by other modeling programs.

There are three basic "tools" in Sculptypaint, which can be used to create a variety of common sculpties:

- Flower Tool
- Stone Tool
- Arch Tool
- Stairs Tool
- Drawing Tool

These tools are displayed as buttons, and each can create specific objects. These tools will be covered in the following sections.

Using the Flower Tool

The flower tool provides a way to create sculpty flowers. Figure 7.2 shows the flower tool in action.

Figure 7.2: Flower Tool

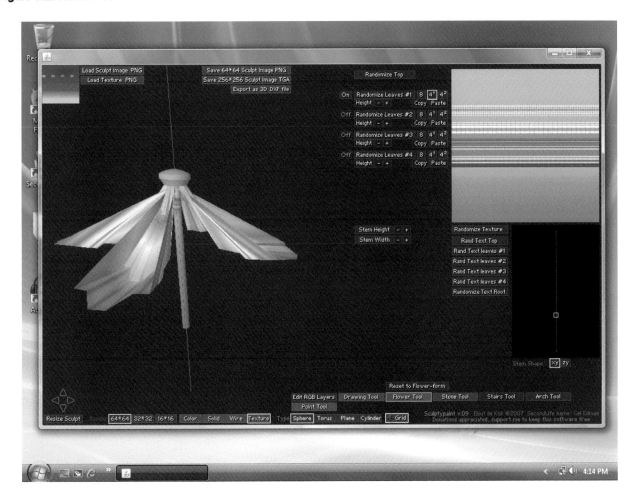

The flower tool allows you to change many of the parameters of a flower. As the parameters are changed, the flower takes shape. The stem height, as well as settings for the individual petals can be specified. To create a flower, click the "Flower Tool" button and then select the "Reset to Flower-form" option that will appear just above the flower tool.

Using the Stone Tool

The stone tool allows you to create somewhat random sculpties that appear as stone or crystal. The stone tool is also useful for resetting an object back to a basic geometric shape, such as a torus, sphere, plane, or cube. Figure 7.3 shows the stone tool in action.

Figure 7.3: Stone Tool

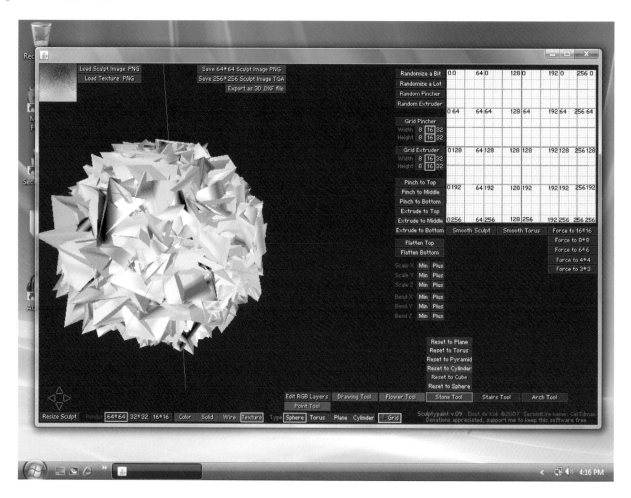

To begin using the stone tool, select one of the "reset" options that will appear just above the "Stone Tool" button. Select the geometric shape that most closely resembles what the final form of the object will look like. The object in Figure 7.3 started out as a cube.

To create the crystal effect, shown in Figure 7.3, the "Randomize a Lot" button was selected. There are many other options which can be selected to extrude and pinch the object, as can also be seen in Figure 7.3. The best way to become familiar with these options is to rotate the object.

Using the Arch Tool

The arch tool allows archways to be created. Figure 7.4 shows the arch tool in action.

Figure 7.4: Arch Tool

To begin creating an archway, select the "Arch Tool" button and then select the "Reset to ArchCube" item that will appear just above it. This will cause a long solid rectangular object to be created that will be bent into an arch. Rotate in one of the dimensions by selecting one of the "Rotate" buttons. Continue increasing the amount of rotation until you are satisfied with the arch. It may be necessary to rotate the object to see that the arch is satisfactory.

Using the Stairs Tool

Prior to sculpties, it was very difficult to create stairs in Second Life. Stairs were generally constructed using of a number of cubes arranged in a stair-like fashion. Quite a few prims were required, usually one for each step. Since landowners are only allowed a limited number of prims per land parcel, stairs were a very wasteful item.

Sculpties have overcome this problem by allowing a staircase to be built using a single prim. Sculptypaint includes a tool specifically designed to create stairs. This tool can be seen in Figure 7.5.

Figure 7.5: Stairs Tool

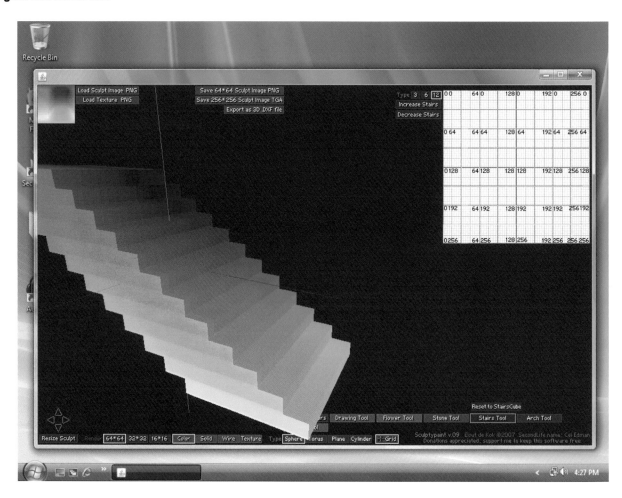

To create stairs, select the "Stairs Tool" and choose the "Reset to StairsCube" option that will appear just above it. This will cause a large cube to be created. Next, select the number of stairs: three, six or twelve. Now, click "Increase Stairs" until the stairs are of the desired height.

Unfortunately, stairs created with the current 0.9 version of Sculptypaint are not terribly useful. They look like stairs, but cannot be used like stairs. This will likely be fixed in future versions. The reason stairs cannot be used, is that avatars are not allowed to physically enter the space of a sculpty. It is helpful to think of each sculpty as being surrounded by an invisible force field. This field is box shaped and it extends completely around the sculpty. The problem with the stairs lies in the way Sculptypaint creates them. The bounding box is larger than it needs to be. If Sculptypaint had used a smaller bounding box, the stairs would be functional. Again, this will likely be corrected in future versions.

Using the Drawing Tool

The drawing tool allows symmetrical free-form modification of a Sculptypaint object. When the drawing tool is selected, the object currently being displayed by Sculptypaint can be edited. Figure 7.6 shows the drawing tool being used.

Figure 7.6: Drawing Tool

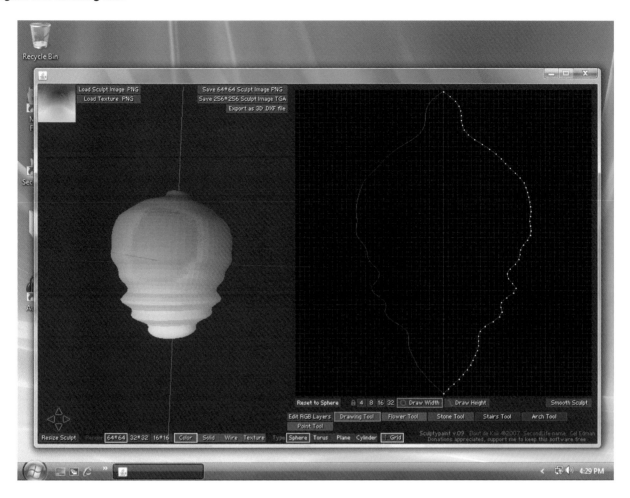

Think of the drawing tool as a lathe. Real world lathes are used to create symmetrical wooden objects, such as chair legs. The drawing tool uses dots to indicate how deeply it will cut the object being modified. By moving the dots, as shown on the right side of Figure 7.6, the object can be sculpted.

From Sculptypaint to Second Life

For this example, the flower created earlier in this chapter will be uploaded to Second Life. To do this, a texture file must first be created. Begin by selecting the "Save 256*256 Sculpt Image TGA" button. This will save the sculpted texture file to the hard drive. Sculptypaint does not allow the filename or location to be chosen. The file will be saved to the same directory in which Sculptypaint resides. There will be two files created for the flower. One is the sculpted image, the other is the texture. The texture image will have "_texture" appended to its name. This file should be uploaded to Second Life. For more information on uploading textures, refer to Chapter 2.

To see the sculpty in Second Life, first create a cube, then edit it. Select the "Object" tab and change the "Building Block Type" to "Sculpted." Next, select the sculpted texture that was uploaded. Finally, select the "Texture" tab and again, choose the texture that was uploaded. Your screen should now look like the screen shown in Figure 7.7.

Figure 7.7: Sculpty Flower in Second Life

The object will now appear as a sculpty.

Summary

The creation of sculpties for Second Life involves very advanced building techniques. An entire book could easily be devoted to sculpty creation. This chapter provides a brief introduction to sculpties. The chapter began by introducing some of the programs that can be used to create sculpties. Most of these programs have fairly steep learning curves and are beyond the scope of this book.

The Sculptypaint program provides a relatively easy way to create sculpties. Sculptypaint includes several tools to create common sculpties for Second Life. This includes stairs, arches, flowers, and stones. Sculptypaint is relatively limited. A more advanced program, Wings 3D, is available and is also commonly used to create sculpties in Second Life.

This is the final chapter of this book. There will likely be future editions as Second Life evolves. We are always looking for suggestions for additional examples to be included future books. If you have any suggestions or comments on this book, feel free to contact us at support@heatonresearch.com.

Heaton Research occasionally schedules classes in the Second Life world. These are almost always free of charge. To keep up to date on our Second Life events, consider joining the Second Life group:

Stop by and visit Heaton Research in Second Life. We own the island of Encogia, which can be found at the following URL:

`http://slurl.com/secondlife/Encogia/197/191/23`

Printed in the United States
101135LV00001B